What if...?

My Story of Panic Attacks

What if...?

My Story of Panic Attacks

by

KC Rinehart

Bright Yellow Hat

What if...? My Story of Panic Attacks
by
K.C. Rinehart

Bright Yellow Hat
an imprint of New Tradition Books
ISBN 1932420436
All rights reserved
Copyright © 2005 by K.C. Rinehart
This book may not be reproduced in whole or in part without written permission.

For information contact:
Bright Yellow Hat
brightyellowhat@yahoo.com

Disclaimer: This book is not intended to replace medical advice or be a substitute for a psychologist. Always seek the advice of a doctor. The author and the publisher expressly disclaim responsibility for any adverse affects of this book. Neither author nor publisher is liable for information contained herein.

For—who else?—those with panic attacks. I know how you feel.

Also for Kris. Thanks for helping me through.

Contents.

Introduction.	1
What if…?	5
As you're reading…	9
The gift of panic:	11
Living in the moment.	25
Acceptance.	27
No rest for the weary.	31
Escape.	34
Use your imagination.	39
Redirecting yourself?	41
Reading material.	43
My visit with a psychologist.	46
Obsessive thoughts.	49
No alternative.	54
The Big Bad.	56
Fear is a four-letter word.	57
The easy guide.	66
The last time I panicked.	68
Life after panic.	72
Knock wood.	78
Exposing yourself to the elements.	81
The biggest fear of all—death.	85
The "reason" for panic?	90
Get back.	94

Introduction.

This is my story of how I dealt with panic attacks. Panic attacks were with me day and night for about two years. Your attacks may have been with you for less time, maybe even more. However, it doesn't matter how long you've experienced these living hells. They can be overcome and you can get back to your life. I am witness to that. They held me down for a long time but, strangely enough, I came to realize that they also helped me.

Yeah, you heard me right. Panic attacks helped me. They taught me some valuable lessons and made me appreciate life more than I ever had before. I'll get more into this in a later chapter, but right now, I want you to know that if you can get over your attacks, your life is going to be good. It might even be better than it was before you got panic attacks. It's hard to imagine right now but it *is* possible.

First of all, I am going to tell you my story, then I am going to break it down in later chapters, taking you step-by-step into what I went through and with my fight with panic. I am going to give you the details so that perhaps it can help you to overcome your panic attacks. While I am not a psychologist, I believe that my experiences can help others. I am just an ordinary person who went through this. These are only my thoughts and my opinions. Take it for what you may but know that *it is only applicable to my own personal experiences.*

I know as you read this, some of the information might unsettle you. That's because when you're having panic attacks, you fear anything can set one off. Just hold tight as you read and try to stay calm. It is my wish that, by the end of this book, you can come to terms with your panic attacks and learn how to stop them.

If you've lived with panic for any length of time, it's easy to lose hope. I know because I, myself, lost hope after a while. Luckily I managed to start going in the right direction. And that's why I wrote this book.

This book is short and to the point. There isn't any "filler" in it. It's also not loaded down with any psychobabble or unnecessary "exercises" and it gets to the point quickly. I know when I was having panic attacks, I would read everything I could get my hands on, hoping to find a cure. Yet, most of the books didn't help and that's because it seemed many of them went around in circles, never getting to the point. By the time the point came across, I was finished with the book, and had given up on trying to figure it out.

What I have done in this book is to just lay out the facts as *I* know them. I'm not asking you to substitute your opinions for my own and that's because I know we all have different experiences when it comes to panic. All I am doing is telling what I have come to believe as the truth—for me. What I did to finally get over panic might not work for everyone. But I believe it will at least give you a little more insight into your problem.

I know many of you out there have been fighting panic for years, maybe even decades, and nothing takes it away. I know the fear you feel as you read this. I know because I was there once. I know how devastating panic can be. I know that feeling of "impending doom" that always seems to float over our heads. I know that feeling of waking up dreading the day because, more than likely, it's going to be a day fighting panic. I know how bleak you life becomes.

I know about the constant "what if" questions that race through your mind, taking you away from your family and friends. I know the "tingly" feeling you get at first when a full-blown panic attack comes on. I know how it feels to be constantly trying to ward off a panic attack. I know the devastation it can wreak. I know how terrible it makes you feel. I know how easy it is to lose hope when panic steps in and sets up shop.

But I also know that panic can be overcome. I'm not offering you instant gratification. I'm not offering you're a miracle cure. I am just offering what I know worked *for me.*

I am going to be very candid, opening up that chapter in my life when panic began so I can share it in hopes that I might be able to help others. Some of the things I write about I've never shared with anyone. But I know that hearing the stories of real people who've gotten over panic attacks is what helped me the most. And it's only through honesty that we can teach each other. And I plan to be honest.

I hope that my experience can help you to get over your panic attacks.

And isn't it time? Isn't it time to take your life back? Your life may be a mess because of panic. It used to be so good, though, didn't it? Before panic, you were living the life, having fun, enjoying your time on earth. But now your life has turned into a nightmare. You're more insecure. You were never insecure a day in your life before panic, were you? You were out there with the best of them doing what you needed to do. Now all you can do is hope you can get through the day without a panic attack.

Make today that day. Today is the day to take your life back and kick panic to the curb. You're ready to get over panic attacks. You're ready to forget about them; in fact, you can't wait until you can forget about them. You're ready for your life to begin again. If that's what you truly want, get ready. It's time to put it into motion.

What if…?

When a person is in the throes of a panic attack, the question of "what if" comes into play. "What if" becomes the only thing we can think of…

What if…
- I get a panic attack?
- Something happens?
- I die?
- I lose control?
- I hurt someone?
- I hurt myself?
- I run my car off the road?
- I do something completely irrational for no reason?
- I run someone over with my car? Even unknowingly?
- I get a panic attack while out in public?

When you get right down to it, there are a lot of "what ifs" to be concerned about. There are legitimate "what ifs"—such as "What if I lock my keys in the car?" or "What if I forget to pay the phone bill?"—and these "what ifs" help us to keep things in check, to have some order in our lives.

However, panic attacks are concerned with the irrational "what ifs" and those are what rule our lives. In fact, our existence becomes concentrated around "what if". It's all about an imagined something happening that will make us lose control. It's the fear of "what if" and "what might happen" that holds us back, that keeps us locked inside of our houses and our minds. This fear follows us everywhere we go, taints everything we do and drains us emotionally and physically. It's a fear of not knowing what's going to happen—whatever that something is—of not being able to foretell the future. "What if" keeps us in a holding pattern, waiting for that imagined something to happen.

More than likely, what we fear is never going to materialize.

But that doesn't keep panic from disrupting our lives. It doesn't keep us from worrying about it. And, most importantly, it doesn't keep panic at bay. In fact, *nothing* keeps panic at bay. Panic has become our lives. It is what we eat, live and breathe. Everything we do is in conjunction with panic. We can't go here or there because it might set off an attack. We can't do this or that for the same reason. In fact, we can't do anything because of panic, least of all be ourselves. We are no longer ourselves, we are victims of panic. It has officially taken over and resides supreme in our lives. It is the king and we are the humble servant.

If what I am talking about applies to you, it's time to take your life back. Having lived with panic attacks, I know what you're feeling. You're probably even feeling a little nervous reading this. You probably want to put the book down and get away from it. Anything, you think, might set off another attack; even reading a book on panic attacks is enough to bring one on. Your mind is starting to race with the "what if" questions: *What if I read this and it makes it worse? What if it goes too far? What if it's too late?*

Stop right now. Don't give in to it. Take a breath and keep reading. And know that it *can* get better.

You should realize that the most important "what if" question you should ask yourself right now is this: *What if I can get over panic attacks?* Another one would be: *What if I can get my life back?*

I'm here to tell you that you can. But first you have to start questioning why you're having panic attacks. In my opinion, panic happens to us because we become overwhelmed by circumstances, whether it is too much stress or a family disturbance or whatever. Panic forces us to concentrate on something else—panic. "I can't worry about that now; I'm having a panic attack."

You can't get over something without first recognizing what you are going though and then examining the root cause of it. Without first questioning why you're having panic attacks, you can't hope to ever get over them. Once you can begin to slow down and listen to what your mind is trying to tell you, you will soon realize that panic doesn't have to be the boss of you.

One problem is that we resist panic so much that we become concentrated on making sure we don't have another attack. This is near impossible. It's like trying to ward off the evil nemesis at the gate but knowing in the back of our minds that he's going to intrude. That's how panic operates, on fear of the unknown. But instead of confronting our enemy, we hide from him, which, in turn, makes him stronger than he ever was. He's going to attack, we just don't know when or where. And that's how he becomes our king.

Then we have the attack and we start the process over again. We hide from it and resist the very thought of panic and then the next thing we know, we have another attack on our hands. That's how panic operates. You get though one attack and there's usually another one waiting on you. So, therefore, we force the idea of panic out of our minds so much that we never relax enough to understand the root cause.

And the root cause is what I am going to concentrate on.

As you're reading...

Because I have had panic attacks, I know reading this might make you nervous, even to the point of bringing a panic attack on. In fact, right now you might be feeling a little bit tingly at the thought of a book like this. Please keep in mind that it is a temporary discomfort that you're feeling. Keep in mind that you can do this, but you have to stay strong.

If you're going through a severe panic attack phase right now, why not read the book in increments? Perhaps five or ten pages a day? Take it little by little if you have to. Do it at your own pace. No one is forcing you to read it. If you read something that upsets you, put the book down and give it five minutes, then pick it right back up. If you do this, you lessen the fear and the panic loses a bit of control.

Keep that in mind as you read but know this is something you need to do in order to get over panic attacks. Even reading a book is a step in the right direction, and that's what it's all about—taking steps until you get back on the path you most desire.

I know that panic attacks make a person very sensitive to things they might not normally be sensitive to. That's okay. I've been there. If you have to, why not say a little prayer? I have found that helps me in most situations.

Ready? Take a deep breath and try to stay focused on the book. *You are a lot stronger than you think.* You've made it this far, haven't you? Tell yourself this often and it will make the process easier. In fact, you might even enjoy it.

The gift of panic: The complete story of my panic attacks.

In a weird way, panic was a gift for me. It didn't seem like a gift at the time but in hindsight, it was exactly that. Without panic to "show me the way" I can honestly say I'd probably be on drugs or in rehab right now. That's because just before I got panic attacks, I was one depressed individual waiting on something to come along and make me happy, something to change my life for the better. That something never materialized. The fact that it probably never would made the pain even worse. I was starting to use alcohol to ease the pain. Before panic hit me, I was considering using drugs. That's how bad it was.

Thank God drugs are illegal and not readily available.

And why was I even considering using illegal substances to alter my mood? It's because I was depressed. I constantly walked around in a low-level funk. Not that anyone knew. My social mask was of a happy-go-lucky girl who had the world on a string. The people I worked with never saw me in a bad mood and I certainly never confided in them about my feelings or told them about my depression. My friends didn't know either. Neither did my family. No one knew but my husband and me. He was the only one I would let see the "real" me, the one that wasn't very nice or loveable. In fact, she could be a real bitch prone to mood swings. She felt at fault for so many things; felt that she wasn't good enough. She felt left out and slighted a lot of the time. She felt as though the world was ignoring her. She hid her rage against the world and only took it out where it was safe—at home.

It wasn't a happy household, to say the least.

Though my husband knew about my depression, there was nothing he could do about it. That fact didn't keep him from trying, though. He would try to cheer me up by telling me funny stories and jokes; he would try to build my self-esteem by telling me how pretty I was. He would do anything to get me to smile. But I didn't smile. Mostly because my life wasn't going where I wanted it to go and I blamed him and the rest of the world for it. If I could only be the person I wanted to be, I could be happy. Who that person was, exactly, is anyone's guess. All I know was that I wanted to move up in the world and be "somebody", somebody that others liked and admired. I felt like a complete nobody and if I could reach my goals, then I would turn into this other person I was sure I was deep inside. That person was happier and, quite truthfully, a better person than me. All it would take was success and then—ta da!—a newer, better me.

I also thought that nothing was good enough in my life. Not my house or my car or my dog or my clothes or anything. I had a very "all or nothing" attitude. I wanted the finer things in life but I didn't want to wait for them—not that I wasn't willing to work for them. I was willing to sacrifice everything to achieve my goals. I just didn't want to wait. I wanted them right now. I wanted to be liked and to be loved. But at the same time, I was afraid to reach out to anyone lest they see the real me. If they saw the real me, they wouldn't like me very much. As a result, I was what everyone wanted me to be. I was a helper and I was good and kind. I let people take advantage of me just so they'd like me. I was afraid to stand up for myself because I didn't want to offend anyone. I let others walk all over me, all the while hoping for my ship to come in so I could run away and not have to ever deal with any of it again.

I was in constant battle with myself, that's what I was. I was constantly trying to succeed. All the while, I would wonder if it was worth all the trouble I was going to. Every little success I gained didn't make a dent in my depression. Each time I'd achieve something, I'd wonder why it didn't make me feel better about myself. I would also downgrade it and say that it wasn't a "real" success and it wasn't exactly what I wanted. I would turn any success into a failure without even realizing what I was doing. And the reason was because I wasn't happy with myself. In fact, I didn't like, let alone love, myself at all. My feelings were bordering on self-hate.

It was pretty miserable existence I lived. And I lived it readily. I didn't question anything; I merely existed for the one day that I'd succeed. And once I did, then I could really start living. Until then, I would just have to sit tight and wait. I believed that as long as I kept up the façade, while hating myself on the inside, it kept me moving. It kept me going towards my goal. If I got too happy or too comfortable, then I'd really be stuck. Nothing mattered in my life except success.

But it didn't keep me moving. It kept me stuck, contrary to what I believed. Not that I thought about it. Not that I questioned my depression or my unhappiness. No. I accepted that that was just the way I was. I believed I had to be like this until this one great thing—success—happened in my life. Then I could reap the rewards and *really* be happy. Until then, as awful as this may seem, I was content to be miserable. If I was actually happy, then any chance of success would be lost because then I would have "settled".

So, I waited on it, getting more and more miserable until it all blew up in my face and I was *forced* to do something.

When I look back on it now, panic was always with me. There would be times when I would have an ominous feeling of "not being real" or the occasional "what-if" and "worse case scenario". But I did the smart thing when this would happen. I'd get up and redirect myself and then the feeling of panic would go away. As with everything else, I didn't question it. I just wrote it off as a weird feeling. By doing this, I was able to sidestep panic for a long time.

However, one day I wasn't so lucky. It's been almost five years since it happened, but I can remember it like it was yesterday.

I was having a crazy year. I was working full-time, sometimes overtime, and taking nine hours of college classes—math included. In addition to this, I ran the household, buying all the groceries, doing most of the housework, all that. There was also a lot of stuff going on with my family—a divorce and sickness—and I was constantly worrying about them and wondering what I could do to help the various situations. During this year, I don't think I ever stopped moving unless I was asleep. I was going to succeed at all costs, even if it cost me my mental health. I don't think I ever sat down and let my mind just rest. I was constantly doing, worrying and running.

One day, my body and brain had had enough. It all came to a head one Friday night. I was sitting at my kitchen table doing some work and drinking a little too much when I looked up and thought, "What if I've done all this for nothing?"

For no reason that I could understand at the time, I began to feel tingly. All of a sudden, my whole body began to pulsate. It was like I'd had been given a big electric shock or something. Before I could stop it, or even define what was happening to me, I began to feel panic in its full effect.

Suddenly, my world closed in on me. I couldn't breath, my mind was racing with these crazy, obsessive thoughts and I *could not* calm down. I had thoughts of suicide and going insane and hurting others. Just odd, unusual thoughts that made me sick to my stomach to have them. I felt like I was going to throw up. I felt like I was going to have a heart attack because my heart was beating faster than it ever had. I felt like I was going crazy. I thought I was going to die. I even considered going to the emergency room because I thought I *was* dying.

I think the attack went on for over an hour. Once I thought I had it under control, I'd have another obsessive thought and it would keep the panic increasing. Nothing calmed me down. I thought I was either dying or on the verge of a major nervous breakdown. Maybe it was neither of the two. Maybe, just maybe, I was losing my mind. That really scared me.

And that's what it felt like. It felt like I was losing my mind. Every time I tried to get back to calm, the panic would come on stronger and stronger. I finally couldn't take it anymore. I asked my husband to go outside with me and take a walk, though it was late in the night. He complied and we walked a little until I felt better, then I got into bed and curled into a ball and just prayed for it to end. It seemed to take a long time for the prayer to come true, but, mercifully, it did and I fell asleep.

The next morning, I wondered, "What was *that*?" But I didn't give it much thought; it was too scary for that. So, I just wrote it off as a fluke of some kind. Maybe it was something I ate. It might have been all the wine I drank; I had had a little *too* much. I didn't know and I didn't care. I was just glad it was gone. It was over and now I could resume my life.

Yeah, right.

Later in the day, I began to notice how "odd" things looked and really began to feel nervous for no reason. Nothing seemed to be real. I shrugged it off, though it went on for the entire weekend. I went into work on Monday as usual. While I was stopped at the usual red-light, I began to get that tingly feeling again and before I knew it, I was having another panic attack. And I had to go into work! I don't know how I did it, but I pulled myself together and went in. As I chatted with co-workers, I wondered if they could "tell" something was wrong with me. I knew something was wrong but didn't know what. That's because I didn't know what panic attacks were.

The panic attacks continued all day on and off. And I'm not talking a little surge of "fight or flight". I am talking full-on, mind-spinning, nauseating, heart-pounding attacks. All day I fought with them, wondering if I was going crazy and becoming sick at the thought. I don't even know how I got through the day without someone calling me on my erratic behavior. I spent a lot of time in the bathroom, wondering what the hell was wrong with me. I almost went home several times but for some reason, I would not let myself give into it. Something told me that I couldn't let it take me over. Instead, I just fought with the attacks, praying to God that the day would end soon.

Finally, the day ended and I raced home. As I drove, I continued to panic severely. I just knew I was losing my mind and I could not stop the obsessive thoughts from coming. They grew stronger and stronger until the point that I was having a hard time breathing. My chest felt tight and my heart was racing so much I was sure it was going to leap right out of my chest. At one point, I even slapped myself, which may sound erratic, but when you're having a panic attack, you'll do anything to try and stop it. The slap didn't make a dent in it and the panic kept coming.

I began to pray to God to tell me what was happening to me. Soon, a thought occurred: *You're having panic attacks.*

Huh. Panic attacks?

I'd heard of panic attacks, of course, everyone has. But I didn't know exactly what they were or how they felt, as this was the start of mine.

I finally made it home and, once there, I got on the internet and started looking up panic attacks. After a few minutes, I was able to confirm the answer to my prayer and had diagnosed myself. I *was* having panic attacks. I was being attacked with panic. I was being attacked. Good. Now that I knew what they were, I could do something about the situation.

For some reason, I thought that the realization of what was happening was enough to cure it. Unfortunately, not so, and I continued to have panic attacks.

And that's what they were—they were attacks. I could be standing in line at the grocery store and I would feel my skin start to tingle and my heart start to pound. I would know panic was on the way and there was no way to outrun it.

The attacks would come at me whenever and wherever they wanted. They didn't discriminate. I couldn't control them. They controlled *me*. I was afraid to get an attack in public, so I began to stay home more. I wouldn't do anything that might set one off. My whole world begin to diminish in scale and became smaller and smaller as I lived inside of chaos.

This went on for *two years.* Stop and think about how long two years is. I'll tell you how long it is: One-hundred and four weeks, seven-hundred and thirty days and a lot of hours and minutes that I spent dedicated to fighting off panic attacks, that I spent being afraid of my own shadow. I couldn't sleep and I couldn't eat and I began to look gaunt and tired and all I thought about was when and where I'd get attacked again.

I was a walking, talking phobic mess. I tried not to let it show. In fact, only my closest family members knew about my panic attacks. I was afraid if I told anyone else they would think I was "crazy".

I tried everything to get "rid" of the panic attacks. When they came at me, I would try to change my thought pattern. That helped a little, but most times they caught me off guard. I went to my regular physician and told him I was having panic attacks. He wrote me a prescription and sent me on my way. Of course, I wouldn't take the drugs he prescribed because I worried that they might make things worse. I went to a psychologist to find out if I was, indeed, crazy. She just confirmed that I was having panic attacks. Other than that, she wasn't helpful at all. She, too, wanted me to go on medication. So, I didn't go back to see her. I tried meditation and yoga, but was afraid if I got *too* relaxed I'd lose control and freak out. I was afraid that anything—from drinking wine to taking an *aspirin*—would set me off and I'd totally lose it and do something bad.

Over time, I began to realize that what set panic off the most were these things called *obsessive thoughts*. Obsessive thoughts are simply thoughts that pop into your head at any time. It might be, "What if I run my car off the road?" or "What if I hurt someone?" Everyone has these occasionally. People who don't have panic attacks know to just let the thought go. People with panic attacks grab onto the thought and succumb to the fear and really believe that they are capable of such things. Other thoughts included, "I must be crazy" and "What if I do this or that and lose control?" and "What if I freak out?" and the all-time favorite, "What if I hurt someone?"

Obsessive thoughts keep us from confronting our fears because it paints fear with a different brush. We can't think about what *really* frightens us, so we come up with other things that aren't based in reality. These things are terrifying but they are nothing more than diversions to confronting what really scares us. They make us believe we will lose control. And after the obsessive thought comes the panic attack.

It's a vicious cycle.

What I realized was that I was afraid of losing control. If I lost control, who knew what I would do? I could hurt someone! I could hurt myself! I could lose control and be put in an insane asylum! To some, these things might seem silly and overdramatic. Why would someone just "do something bad" for no reason? But that's the way panic works. It's part paranoia and part self-punishment. You begin to believe in what panic tells you and it tells you to run and to hide. It also tells you that nothing can ever take it away and that's because it perpetuates itself. The more you give in, the stronger it becomes and the smaller your world gets.

And my world got pretty small. Every prospect seemed like an opportunity for panic to wreak havoc on me. I was miserable. I stopped laughing. I stopped enjoying food. I stopped enjoying the company of others. I stopped going places and looking forward to the holidays. I stopped sleeping at night. I would lie awake, staring at the ceiling, feeling helpless to do anything. I would cry and pray and wonder why this was happening to me. In essence, I stopped living. I stopped it all because panic had won.

I was no longer concerned about succeeding or being a perfect employee or a good friend or a good wife. I didn't care about getting my college degree or achieving my goals. I was just concerned about getting through the next day. All I felt was this impending doom rising over my head and threatening to fall and suffocate me. Panic was like an ongoing nightmare, one that I couldn't awake from, one that I might not ever escape. I awoke feeling dread and went to sleep—if I was lucky to be able to actually fall asleep—feeling dread. I dreaded the fact that the panic would attack again. I wondered if I'd get out of without doing something "crazy". It was a discomfort with life in general. It was misery at its finest.

The only person I could really talk to during all of this was my husband and, while he tried to help by offering me suggestions on how to stay calm and by just listening to me, there wasn't much else he *could* do. I was lucky that I had him, but at the same time, I felt very alone in the world. I felt like I was the only one who had ever gone through this. I felt like I was being punished for being such a "bad" person. And though I was far from being "bad", I felt bad and I felt like panic was my comeuppance.

It wasn't pretty, to say the least. And all of this because I refused to take a break. I kept putting stress on myself and this was the thanks I got. I had cultivated misery and now I was more miserable than I could ever imagine. Lucky me.

After two years of living in this perpetual hell, something suddenly changed. It changed because one day the fog broke and I could see what was going on. And it happened because I got mad. I had been fighting with panic all day and I was just so *tired* of it. I was starting to get angry at it so, I started asking questions: How could this happen to me? I was a good person. I treated people well. I tried to eat my vegetables and if I hurt someone's feelings—like my husband's—I would feel enormous guilt for days. I just had to make sure I was punishing myself. What did I do wrong? Sure, I wasn't perfect, and I had made mistakes, but I was human. Humans make mistakes. Why was I being punished?

But the fact of the matter was, I wasn't being punished, I was being shown the way.

I took off from work early that day and went home and sat on the couch. I refused to move off of it until I could make some sense of all this. While I don't consider myself to be overtly religious, I do believe in God, so I began to pray. I prayed, "God, please just help me." I prayed this over and over and then I would stop and take a breath. I knew it was going to be hard, but I had to do it. I was also scared to death that I might go crazy but I thought, *So what? If they have to take me away in a straightjacket, then that's what they'll have to do.* I couldn't live like this anymore. I had to have some answers and only God could help me.

I then remembered something I had read about psychosomatic disorders and wondered if it would apply to panic attacks as well. The theory is that when people have psychosomatic disorders, whether it's a bad back or constant sinus trouble, it's just really the body's way of slowing down when the mind is faced with a threat, like being a failure or working too hard and having too much stress. So, we bury our fears and just deal with the physical pain instead. However, if you face up to your fears, your pain will usually go away.

It sounded like a plan to me. This is what I had to do: Face my fears and stop panic in its tracks. And that's what I did. I was going to face up to it. But I didn't know what my fear was. So, I asked God to help me: *"Please, God, just let me know what it is."* And, I swear, it was like a miracle. The first thought in my head was this: "I am afraid of being a failure."

I instantly knew that was it. I was afraid of being a failure. I was afraid of not being good enough. I was so afraid of it, I drove myself into the ground, working crazy hours and doing everything in my power to "get ahead". Nothing was more important to me than success. I had to have it! I worked hard for it. I *deserved* it.

So you see, when I had that thought of, "What if I've done all this for nothing?" I had just confronted my deepest fear. Instead of dealing with it, I succumbed to panic and began to think obsessive thoughts such as "I must be crazy" and "What if I do this or that and lose control?" As I said, these thoughts are terrifying but they are nothing more than a diversion from confronting what *really* scares us. That's why I had tell myself, "If I go crazy, they can just take me away in a straightjacket" first before I could get to the root cause. It's almost like I had to accept the worse-case scenario before I got to the real fear. Once I accepted it, I could accept my greatest fear and get past it.

In essence, all I did was retrace my panic back to where it initially started, there at the kitchen table. And I had to tell myself that whatever happened once I figured it out would be fine. I accepted the imagined consequences before

I could face the real fear. Once I did that, I found the fear that forced panic on me and faced it. After I did this, I wondered why I had let it get to me.

That was easy to figure out. It got to me because it was my deepest fear, being a failure. It scared me to death. The only thing I thought I could do was to run away from it. I ran so hard to get away from that thought, I ran right into panic's arms. And it embraced me. It smothered me for two years. But dealing with the panic was much easier than confronting my fear and facing my inadequacies.

But I did eventually deal with it. I stared my fear right in the face and let the thought that I might be a failure sink in. And you know what? It wasn't so bad. In fact, it was liberating. Once I faced it, an enormous weight lifted off my shoulders. I felt like I had been carrying a railroad tie on my shoulders for two years and all of a sudden, it was like God had reached down and plucked it off. I know it sounds hokey, but it was like a religious experience. I had never felt as good in all of my life as I did at that moment.

It sounds almost too simple, doesn't it? But it's true. I was afraid of not being liked and of not being perfect and of not reaching my goals and of being a failure. That little fear chased me like a hellhound for two years. It made my life absolutely miserable. I realized I hadn't been living for me; I had been living for my fears and for other people. I let other people's opinions mold me into this scared, little creature. I was afraid if I said I was cracking under the pressure they would look at me like I was deranged.

I used to worry about being perfect. I was anal-retentive and it all blew up in my face when I was forced to face up to my inadequacies. I was such a control freak that I would wig out if my husband did something as insignificant as leaving something in the middle of the floor, like a pair of socks. I couldn't deal with all this and his socks, too! I would yell and scream at him at any opportunity. Now, not so much. Now, if he leaves socks in the middle of the floor, he can walk over them until he picks them up. Now I don't yell and scream so much anymore. It's not worth the effort. The little things are just that—little things.

And that's why I decided to reorganize my life and get some of the stress out. If I hadn't gotten panic attacks, I might have had a full-fledged nervous breakdown. It showed me how silly things really are. It showed me my endless worries about the future and about success weren't important. It showed me how to live in the moment because, when you're having a panic attack, you can't help *but* live in the moment.

After I finally got over panic attacks, I was able to start living. All that stuff that held me down didn't matter anymore. All that mattered was living, loving and learning about myself and others. My whole world opened up and I began to try things I would have never dreamed about trying before. I tasted new foods and I saw new places. Not only that, but I had the courage to let go of people who drained me emotionally, the ones who only wanted to use me. Panic gave me the courage to do these things.

Without panic, I would still be living in a small world, waiting for happiness to come and find me. Now I know that happiness just doesn't find a person, nor can a person go looking for it. I've found that happiness is really simple and easy. It's not this huge thing, happiness, and it's not the answer to all our prayers. Happiness is simply living your life in the moment and enjoying your time. Happiness is simply being in a good mood. That's all it is. And without panic, I would have never realized this. And that's why I say it was a gift.

Living in the moment.

Does it still happen, though? Sometimes, yes, I do feel the start of a panic attack. And once I do, I know what to do in order to deal with it. And all I do is face my fear.

For me, panic has become a test. For instance, I went on a cruise recently and once we got on the boat, I almost had a panic attack. I couldn't imagine staying on that boat for seven days! I almost freaked out and ran off it. But I stopped myself, sat down with a soda and told myself that if anything happened, then I could get off but right now, I was going to live in the moment. It worked and I had a great time and not an incident of panic after that. Sure, it was hard, especially when the boat began to pull away from the dock, but I just concentrated on myself and watched the water until I felt the nervousness dissipate. I asked myself what I was afraid of and thought, "I'm afraid I might freak out on the boat." I told myself that was okay and to take a breath. Then I took it moment by moment and once I did that, I was able to get over the panic.

You have to keep in mind that if you give into panic all the time by running off a boat or whatever, then it wins. You *have* to challenge it. And once you start, then you can be free of it. Sure, it might rear its ugly head every now and then but when you feel it, just ask yourself what you're afraid of and let it come to you. Once you do, you'll realize it's not that big of a deal. Remember that you are always bigger than your fear.

Panic is fear. It feeds on the fact that it knows you're going to run away and hide. It wants you to be miserable. But it is possible to stop it and all you do is face fears as they come. And you do that by always living in the moment. Stop worrying about "what you might do" and get through that first bit of discomfort and it will usually dissipate on its own. Another thing to be aware of, as I've said, is that we always try to resist panic. I've found that the more I try to resist it, the harder it comes on. But, if I just live in the moment, panic loses its grip.

And that's all there is to it. Face the fear as it comes and deal with it. If you can come up with an immediate solution—like staying on the boat—then do it. If not, wait it out and let what you're afraid of occur to you. If you can just force yourself to think rationally and realize that you've been through this before and you survived, it will help you to understand that you can do it again. You can handle it. I have found this works in most situations Give it a try.

Acceptance.

One thing that you need to do before you do anything else is to accept that you are having panic attacks. If, for some reason, you're not sure this is what you're experiencing, it's a good idea to see someone—a therapist, a psychologist, etc.—to get diagnosed. It is also a good idea to see a regular physician to make sure that you're not suffering from a medical condition. I know a lot of people think they're having heart attacks when they have their first major panic attack. While they're not having a heart attack, they still need to get checked out by a doctor. It never hurts to be too careful.

So how do you know for sure that you're having a panic attack? Well, there shouldn't be any doubt but if you feel a sudden surge of nervous energy accompanied by heart palpations, sweating, nausea and mind racing, then you're probably having a panic attack. One of the biggest things is that you feel like you're losing control. Your "fight or flight" instinct also kicks in. Should you stay and fight or should you run? With panic, we usually want to run.

It's important to understand the fight or flight response when dealing with panic. This response is innate and it is our body's way to prepare us to fight or flee from a perceived attack or threat. It's this response that triggers the nerves and gives us those "tingly" feelings and fires up our adrenaline. Essentially, our body prepares itself for a fight or to flee. We began to "scan" and seek out potential dangers and our fear becomes exaggerated.

With panic and our instinctual fight or flight response, we begin to see everything through fear. Everything becomes a potential threat. Panic really kicks this on and that's why we stop being able to relax and start just trying to survive moment to moment. We live from one panic attack to the next, never stopping to enjoy a moment's peace.

Of course, many of us don't know that this is what's happening to us. Like I said, it's always best to see a professional to make sure. *Never* hesitate to get diagnosed. It's always a step in the right direction and no shame should ever be attached to it.

As I will talk about in a later chapter, I hesitated to see a psychologist because, being from a small town—and around small-minded individuals—I feel that there's a certain stigma attached to seeing a professional. No one wants to be labeled "crazy". I certainly didn't either and I might have set myself back months because I refused to see someone at first. When it comes to panic attacks or any other medical condition, *your health is much, much more important than the opinion of others.* Always keep that in mind and make your recovery the most important thing in your life.

Another thing to keep in mind when you're having panic attacks is that it's not your fault and you're not being "punished". Sure, you might try to blame yourself by wondering what you "did wrong" that caused you to bring this on yourself, but you haven't done anything wrong. I know you might feel this way because I felt that way from time to time: "What did I do to deserve this? It must have been something really, really bad." I would pick my past apart, trying to find that one thing that might have set all this off. I couldn't find it because that wasn't the case.

You need to realize that panic occurs for numerous reasons, but there's really no sense in trying to blame to it on yourself. I know that some people get panic attacks because of stress or situations beyond their control or things that happened in their childhood or drug use but, in my opinion, most seem to get them because of a fear they possess. That's why I got mine, as I discussed in the previous chapter.

The most important thing to keep in mind is that you have panic disorder and that you're not crazy. It's hard not to think that because of all the irrational thoughts a person has when they experience panic, but try to keep this in mind. In fact, believe it because it's true.

Let me reiterate: Accept that while you are having panic attacks, it doesn't mean you're losing your mind. Panic happens to us because of fear and situations beyond our control.

Always keep in mind, too, that awareness is a big part of it. Take note of what triggers an attack, ascertain the reason. The thing with panic is that the fears we develop are learned. We learn to be afraid of certain things and situations. In effect, we teach ourselves to be afraid. When this happens, panic makes us begin to doubt ourselves. Once the doubt enters, panic makes itself right at home. Certain things, of course, will trigger the fears. It might be thinking about jumping out of a plane or watching the news and seeing a report on something catastrophic. Regardless, it has the same effect. It's our job to be aware of it and learn to recognize the triggers and stop associating them with panic. Think of it this way: Once, you weren't afraid of doing something but now you are and that's because you've taught yourself to be afraid of it. And you can un-teach yourself. It takes some work, but it can be done.

One last thing. Some people think that panic is inherited. While I am not going to dispute that, I do think it has some bearing, so it might be a good idea to call someone in your family and ask if anyone else has had panic attacks. If nothing else, it might give you a little more clarity on the issue. The first person I called after I found out I was having panic attacks was my mother. The first words out of her mouth were, "Oh, no, not you too."

My mother suffers from panic attacks as well as one of my aunts. I believe my mother's panic comes from a car wreck we had when I was small. None of us were hurt, but it really jarred her because she had all of her children in the car when it happened. She still fears driving, mainly because she fears that she will experience a panic attack while she's driving. So she does it at her own pace.

Knowing you're not the only one can also be a comfort. It was to me. You might be able to gain some insight by listening to someone else's story. You might even be able to help them.

No rest for the weary.

Nobody knew about my panic attacks. No one knew except my husband, my mother and my sister. That's because I thought if they knew, they'd think I was "crazy". I didn't tell anyone I worked with because I was scared they'd fire me over it. I didn't tell my friends because I didn't want them to abandon me.

I didn't tell anyone because, to tell the truth, I didn't understand what was happening to me. I just knew that my world had toppled. In fact, it had crashed down on me.

Before panic I was trying too hard. I was trying so hard to be perfect, too hard to succeed. I was trying too hard at everything all the while neglecting my own well-being. After a while, all this began to take its toll. It chewed me up and broke me down. I believe that's one reason I began to have the attacks. The odd thing about it is that, while I was consumed with trying to do better and be better, during an attack, my well-being was the furthest thing from my mind. I just wanted to live through it.

Panic squeezed every bit of joy out of my life until I was a shell of my former self. People I hadn't seen in years might not have recognized me on the street. I usually appeared to be fairly happy-go-lucky. Now I was gaunt, tired, restless. I couldn't eat and nothing mattered but staving off another attack. The days were long and panic filled. But getting through the day was nothing compared to getting through the night.

Something else panic took away from me was a good night's rest. Panic doesn't discriminate between night and day. It can come at any time. It's especially scary at night. Before panic, I slept like a baby and I always looked forward to getting into bed and curling up and sleeping. Every night I made sure to get my eight hours. I even loved taking naps when I could. Sleep, for me, was a comfort, it was a guilty pleasure. There's nothing like being well-rested. After panic, I was lucky to get three or four hours a night. And that was on a good night. Most nights I didn't sleep at all. I'd lie awake, staring at the ceiling and praying that the things that go "bump" in the night wouldn't get me. I'd lie there and pray that I didn't suddenly get an urge to do something "bad". I'd lie there and shake and panic and want to cry.

After I got over panic, I still felt a little uneasy about falling asleep. And that's because when you fall asleep you give up control of yourself and, as we all know, if you suffer from panic attacks, this is almost unbearable. We think we might "do" something in our sleep. Giving ourselves over to dreamland is a nightmare because... *What if something happens when I'm asleep? What if I do something when I'm asleep and don't even realize it?*

It took a lot of practice but after a while, I was able to get back to my normal sleeping pattern. I'd go to bed and read until I couldn't hold my eyes open and then I'd fall asleep. If I woke up with a panicky feeling—which was rare—I would calm myself down, close my eyes and force myself to go back to sleep. I did this until it became second nature again. I knew I couldn't give in to the fear otherwise it would be that much harder to deal with it later. So what if I woke up feeling shaky? Then I woke up, that's all! I also accepted the imagined consequences if I "did" something at night. If it happened, it happened, nothing I can do about it. I gave up control when it came to sleep and it worked to help me get back into bed and snoozing.

It also helped my well-being. Getting enough sleep is one of the most important things we can do for our health.

Panic takes so much out of us. It takes our rest away and our mental well-being. It also takes the wind out of us. After an attack, I felt like I'd been in a fight for my life and, really, that pretty much sums it up. You are in a fight for your life, trying to gain control back, trying to get through it to see the other side.

And you can. You can do it.

Panic is terror. But it can be stopped. One thing I wished I'd realized earlier is that when you're having a panic attack, it's just a momentary discomfort, like having a rock in your shoe or something. Get through the moment, retrace back to the start of the panic attack and find the obsessive thought/fear. If you can make this a habit, then you stop panic in its tracks. I'll get more into this idea a little later in the book.

Escape.

That's what we're all afraid of not having, aren't we? An escape. With panic, one always has to be on the lookout for a possible escape.

Sometimes, there's not one available.

As I mentioned in an earlier chapter, I recently went on a cruise. I was going to be on a big boat for seven whole days. I was fine when I walked onto the ship but once it started pulling away from the dock, I almost freaked out.

You have to understand that you can't put your life on hold because of panic. By doing things that you wouldn't normally do and taking chances, you give yourself less reason to doubt yourself. Once you can begin to do things that you once enjoyed again, like riding on a plane, your self-confidence will grow.

However, it's taking that one big step that's the hardest, isn't it? Believe me, I know this. But after you take that one big step, all the others will seem less intimidating. And all you have to do is *just do it*. Some will say to tap into your self-confidence or whatever, but I say most of us can't find that self-confidence at that moment. It's lost in the panic.

Let me reiterate: Don't think, just do. Of course, your mind will be racing, your heart will be pounding, but don't let it deter you. *Force* yourself out the door, into the car. Force yourself to drive. Force yourself to do what you're most afraid of doing, even if it's just going to see a horror movie or swallowing a pill. Force it. Once it's done, relief will sweep over you.

You have to keep in mind that no one can really help you to overcome your fears. You have to care enough about yourself to get over them. You have to take care of yourself and part of taking care of yourself is making yourself do something you know deep in your heart you should do.

If you can force yourself to do whatever it is you need to do—those ordinary everyday tasks such as plane rides, driving, whatever—you will free yourself and you'll wonder why you didn't do it sooner. Always remember it's just fear that keeps you from taking "chances". If you force yourself to do something and then inevitably come out of it okay, you'll have conquered your fear.

That's what I did. I had to force myself to start doing things, without the confidence. And once I did them, my confidence started coming back until I stopped thinking every little thing was going to set off an attack. But without initially forcing myself, I wouldn't have done it, confidence or no confidence. I just had to make up my mind that I was going to do things and once I took that first big step, all the other steps were smaller and more manageable. If you can force yourself into taking that first big step, you'll win over panic. It can't stick around to torment you if you don't always give into it. Eventually, it will dissolve on its own, but it's up to you to take that first big step to make it go away.

Always keep in mind that with anything, including panic, that first big step is going to be the hardest. You will probably tell yourself that you "can't" do it, but, of course, you can. Tap into whatever you have to tap into to get through it. If it's self-confidence or willpower or even spite, do it. Yes, spite. If you can spite yourself into doing something, that's just as good a way to take that step as any. If you have to get pissed off at yourself, then do it. Do it *in spite* of what you tell yourself. "I will do this and nothing will stop me." Tap into your anger. Tap into whatever it is you have to tap into to take that step. You have a wide array of emotions to pull from. Use them, that's what they're there for.

Whatever works for you, use it to your advantage. Also, keep in mind that you are a lot stronger than you'd ever give yourself credit for. If you've been having panic attacks and have "gotten" through them, you've definitely shown the world your strength, endurance and resilience. Getting through a panic attack of any scale is a feat. Use that when you get ready to take your big step. Say to yourself that you've been through the wringer and if you're on the other side of it, nothing can stop you. And it's true.

One reason we have such a problem taking those steps is because panic distorts reality. You look at people you know very well and ask yourself who, precisely, they are. Where did they come from? Why are they there with you? You look at things, objects, and see their shape. You begin to really hear the little things in the world, like a car door opening or the creaking sound of a door that needs to be oiled. Your senses are alert and ready to seek out potential dangers. You become conscious of everything and nothing escapes your awareness. It's almost like watching an intense movie—all the time.

I can remember being in a fast-food restaurant right after I started having panic attacks and my senses were hyper-sensitive. I could hear the drink machine kick on; I could hear someone opening a ketchup pack near me. I could hear the change rattle in the cash register. It's like you become slowly aware of everything. Panic does make the world come into focus and that's because we're focusing on everything, looking for a possible threat, for something that might set the panic off.

It's my opinion that panic is carried over from generations of hunters and gatherers. Back then, people needed panic to get away from a threat—maybe a wild animal—which means they needed it in order to survive. It was a survival tool. Panic is brought into focus so you can prepare yourself for escape, just like our ancestors had to do so they could get away from a threatening situation. That's why you feel that surge of sudden energy, that adrenaline rush. Think about it. Right before an attack starts, don't you feel just alive and ready to run? And that's because you are. Your body is readying itself to run away from a threat. The only problem is, with panic, the threats are normally harmless. They're imagined. Panic mixes up the signals and we start running for no reason.

It is basic "fight or flight", as I talked about in an earlier chapter. During our ancestors' times, a person had to ascertain whether they were going to stay and fight or run. Now, with panic, we don't even think about fighting, we run at the slightest inclination.

And that's why it usually wins and takes over our lives.

Next time, stay and fight with it. See it through to the end. Don't leave a situation early. Question it. Call it onto the carpet and tell it to make itself known.

Another problem with panic is the uncertainty it places in our lives. As I mentioned before, things that we once enjoyed become alien, even our family. Nothing seems familiar. Anything makes us nervous. We might begin to look at people a certain way and wonder why our heads are shaped the way they are. We might wonder why we walk the way we walk or why we have to sleep or eat. (I once thought about food and how, once ingested, it just disappears. That was a very strange thought.) We might concentrate on sounds more, listening for things that aren't there. And, as I said, I think we're built to do this in order to ascertain potentially threatening situations. With panic, every situation becomes potentially threatening.

What we have to do is recognize what we're doing. That's all. Yes, there is a reason we all have our "spider senses" and our intuitions, and we should always tap into them. But we have to weed out the threat and we have trust in ourselves to do that. Once we can begin to do that, panic will usually dissipate on its on. And that's what we're after, right?

Use your imagination.

People prone to panic attacks have one thing in common: They've all got great imaginations. In fact, many of us have over-active imaginations. Without it we wouldn't be able to come up with the imagined circumstances we do.

It's a blessing, this gift of imagination, but when you're having panic attacks, it becomes a curse.

Try this: When you find your imagination taking over and leading you down the panic path, switch gears on it and use it to your advantage by imagining something nice, like a pretty beach or a good meal you'd like to eat soon. All you're doing is changing your thought process. Once you can do that, you can stop these thoughts, if you just practice. You can turn it around. It takes a bit of work, but you can do it.

If you can't do that, switch your focus to a good book or to the TV. Another good thing to do is to listen to music. Keep a favorite CD around and when you feel a bit panicky, put it on and get lost in the music. Do anything so you don't give into panic. Soon, it will become like second nature and you'll wonder why you let it bother you in the first place. It really works. I've done it myself.

Another thing we panic attack sufferers do is over-identify with everyone else in the world. Sure, being concerned and caring is great, but we take it a step further. No matter what it is, we feel other people's pain. We can't watch the news because someone might be hurt and that hurts us too, doesn't it? We fixate on others so much, over-identifying with their problems, all the while thinking, "Oh, God, what if that was me?" That thought makes us feel guilty and that makes us even more susceptible to panic. So we punish ourselves with a little panic.

One way to force yourself to stop over-identifying is to just listen to others' problems, sympathize and then learn to let it go. It's takes a bit of work but you can do it. All you have to do is set a limit to how much you're going to make yourself "suffer"—and that's all you're really doing—then force yourself to stop. It's almost like you're picking on yourself. So, stop picking on yourself.

Redirecting yourself?

When you're having panic attacks, some people will tell you to simply redirect the panic. That means, when you feel one coming on, start doing an unrelated task immediately and get so involved in it that the panic dissipates on its own.

Yes, this does work but it is my opinion that it will only work for a while. The panic that you're feeling is probably caused by a deep-seated fear you possess. The thing I had to realize was that it wasn't about sidestepping the panic but about *facing the fear that gave me the panic in the first place.*

There are many methods to controlling panic and I'm not going to discredit any of them. I realize that different things work for different people. All I know is that, for me, the root cause of my panic was my greatest fear. Redirection wouldn't help with that. Drugs wouldn't either, for that matter.

Yes, for some people, anti-anxiety drugs *are* the answer. If you have severe panic attacks, they might be the only solution. *I'm not telling anyone to get off their medicine.* However, I do believe that, in our society, too many doctors just throw medicine at a problem. Why not treat the root cause? That is much more likely to bring about a cure. Medicine, in my own personal opinion, usually just treats the symptoms, not the problem.

The question to ask the doctors is: What happens once we get off the medicine? Will the panic return? Who knows? Hopefully, it won't, but there's no guarantee. It's my opinion—*and my opinion only*—that medication is nothing more than an attempt to redirect the panic. If this is the case, then what happens to the panic? Doesn't the panic have to go somewhere if it's redirected? Where does it go? Does it stay there, waiting to come out if you skip a pill?

That's a hard pill to swallow, no pun intended.

If you can get to the root cause of the panic, you won't have to worry about redirecting yourself and you won't have to worry about taking pills for the rest of your life. Sure, it might not work for everyone, but it worked for me. It took me two years to finally figure this out. I didn't need medicine, though my doctor wanted me to take it. I didn't need redirection. I needed to face my fears.

Let me say it again: *Getting to the root cause will get you closer to the cure.* I truly believe this. We don't need more medicine; we need to help others help themselves. Cures rarely come in pill form. They come from understanding and from the willingness to do something for ourselves. It takes courage to look deep inside and face fear. A pill can't give you that. Courage is the only thing that can.

Yes, you can learn to redirect yourself to stave off a panic attack. But if you never get to the root cause of why you're having them, you'll have to sidestep them the rest of your life. You will always have that little fear eating at you, threatening to turn into a full-blown attack. It's terrifying, I know. But, if I can do it, anyone can.

Reading material.

While I was having panic attacks consistently—about four to seven a day—I was desperate to find help and I looked everywhere, trying to clue into a magic potion or cure that might make it all go away. I searched in vain for that elusive thing that would make things right again. I soon realized that no matter where I went, no one seemed to have the answers.

I visited message boards on the internet—big mistake. I say this mainly because the situations people wrote about made me feel even *more* panicked. I thought *I* had it bad. Some of those people had it worse than I could ever imagine. It didn't take long for me to realize that the message boards were making a dire situation even more stressful. So I moved on to books.

In the beginning, I bought so many books that I could have opened a library for panic attacks. I kept buying them, looking for that one thing that would help me through this nightmare. I read everything I could get my hands on about panic attacks. Again, I found that nothing helped much. Sure, some of the books were okay but most were written by people—psychologists—who had never had a panic attack in their lives.

The main problem I had with these books was that they all told me to "learn to live with the panic". Like it was an enemy I could turn into a friend or something. Learn to live with it? Why would I *want* to do that? Why would I want to learn to live with something that kept me terrified at all times? Something that made sure I didn't enjoy a good night's sleep? Something that made me look gaunt and tired all the time? Something that sucked every bit of joy out of my life? How was that living?

Sure, the advice they offered was sound and good, but it didn't take away the panic. It seemed as though *nothing* could take the panic away. One book I read even went as far to say those very words. It told me that once I had panic in my life, I would always have panic and all I could do was learn to live with it. This made me feel absolutely hopeless. I realized that the books weren't helping and I began to feel even more helpless, even more desperate. Was I going to have to live with panic for the rest of my life?

I didn't want to. I had lived without it for a long time, so why did I have to learn to live with it now? Why did I have to rearrange my world in order to accommodate it? Wouldn't that mean I would have to deal with it for the rest of my life? I didn't want to deal with panic attacks for the rest of my life. I wanted them to leave me alone. I didn't want to live with something that made the very thought of going on vacation a nightmare. I didn't want to live with something that took so much out of me I sometimes wondered how I made it through the day. I didn't want to live with something that threatened to rear its ugly head at anytime and ruin my day.

But that's what many of the books told me to do: Learn to live with it. As if I'd eventually get used to it. Sure, there are many things we *can* learn to get used to but panic isn't one of them. No matter how long we have panic attacks they always make us uneasy. An attack never gets any easier and that's because it's unnatural. Being in constant fear of having a panic attack is a very unnatural way to live. It's a constant state of discomfort with the world at large.

No matter how hard I tried to convince myself that I could just "learn to live" with panic, I knew I couldn't. And that's because living with panic is no way to live.

After so many books, I just stopped reading them. They just weren't helping that much. I searched for two years before I began to realize that no one could help me but me. So, I set out to do just that.

My visit with a psychologist.

My panic attacks became so bad that I knew I was going to have to seek professional help. It was a hard decision to make because I thought once I made it, then I'd have to accept the fact that something might really be "wrong" with me. I kept hoping I'd wake up one morning and the panic would miraculously be gone. So, I kept putting off seeing someone about my problem until it escalated to the point that I had no other alternative.

First of all, before going to the psychologist, I went to my regular physician, just to make sure there wasn't anything physically wrong with me. Previously, I had been in to see him because I had been having severe stomach problems, which I now know were caused by stress. I had tests run, blood drawn. He didn't help me with my stomach problems and when I told him I was having panic attacks, I knew he wasn't going to help me with that either.

After I told him, he just gave me this look that said, "Why are you wasting my time with this?" Then he scribbled something down on a notepad and told me to take some drugs. Then he turned on his heel and walked out of the room like I had done him the greatest disservice by asking for his help. After I left his office, I drove around until I found an empty parking lot beside a church and there I burst into tears. I had never, in my life, felt so bad about asking for help. And that's all I had done. That's when I realized that most people who've never had a panic attack don't understand what those of us who have them are going through. Not only that, most of them don't care. It's not their problem, you know?

I never went back to see him after that—ever. I'm amazed this insensitive man is still in business.

A few months after that, I began to consider going to someone who might be more sympathetic—a psychologist. But I didn't want to do it. I hesitated and put it off for months but one day the attacks got so bad that I forced myself to stay in my office for the majority of the day. That was when I finally broke down and looked up a psychologist in the phonebook and made an appointment. Because she couldn't see me right away, I had a few days to think about it, so I broke the appointment.

This became a pattern. I would call, set the appointment up, and then break it. I think I made and broke about five appointments before I finally kept one. I shouldn't have been so hesitant but somehow I knew a psychologist wasn't really going to help me. I don't know why I felt this way because there are many people that psychologists help. Another reason I didn't want to go was because I didn't want the psychologist to tell me I was crazy. That was one of my biggest fears, that I might just be crazy.

But I knew I needed to do it. So, one day in early fall, I found myself in a psychologist's office telling her about my panic attacks. She listened, took some notes, asked some questions, and told me something about "obsessive thoughts". Then she, of course, prescribed me some drugs, telling me there was no alternative but to take them. (Doesn't it seem like this is their answer to everything?)

I told her that I didn't want to take drugs, but she insisted I begin to take some anti-anxiety medication that's very popular now. She didn't know but I couldn't take drugs—any drugs, not even an aspirin. That's how bad my panic attacks were. I refused to take any medicine, sure that it would make me lose control and I'd do something "bad". I thought anything would set me off and here she was prescribing me mind-altering drugs. I didn't think so. This was heavy-duty stuff.

I knew the visit had been in vain. I left her office, shoulders slumped and sat in my car, staring at the prescription. This wasn't going to work for me. I don't have anything against someone using drugs but for myself, I just didn't want to get dependent on anything. And that's if I could force myself to actually take the drugs, which, I knew, I couldn't.

I threw the prescription away and decided that I'd just have to learn to live with the panic on my own. Help wasn't on the way and nobody could do anything to assist me in getting over the panic. Panic was mine and, it seemed, it would always be.

That's the day that I began to give up. That's when hope seemed to disappear. My world was going to get a lot smaller and more confined. There wasn't much I could do about it and, apparently, there wasn't any other alternative. I had tried everything from books to doctors, but nothing helped, nothing took the panic away. It seemed to me, at the time, that panic was here to stay.

Obsessive thoughts.

It took a few days after my visit with the psychologist for what she had said to sink in. She had told me I was having panic attacks which were precipitated by obsessive thoughts.

I didn't even know what obsessive thoughts were.

But for some reason, that term stuck in my head and I wrote it down. I started doing some research and figured out what obsessive thoughts were. Basically, an obsessive thought is a thought that pops into your head that sets off a panic attack. It can be a "bad" thought, perhaps something along the lines of, "I could hurt that person", or "I could run my car off the road".

The most common obsessive thoughts are about things like germs, doubts about your own character, violence and fear. Once an obsessive thought such as this pops up, it seems to repeat over and over and is almost impossible to ignore. It's like the thought is hammering away vividly inside of your mind and your mind begins to race with different scenarios. Not only that, but the thought seems to increase in size and scale and gets worse and worse, which in turn causes more and more anxiety. Once you have one, it becomes the only thing you can focus on and that's because it's an "inappropriate" thought which causes the panic.

Obsessive thoughts are one reason our worlds become small after we get panic attacks. We're afraid we might "do" something or "catch" something or sometime "might happen" to us or whatever. Also, we start looking for things to get rid of, such as knives and books, and we start avoiding situations that might make us have an obsessive thought, such as violent films, the news, etc. We think if we have a knife lying around, we might pick it up and use it. Of course, we won't, it's just the obsessive thoughts make us believe we *could*. This is one reason we begin to think we're "crazy".

It's worth mentioning that everyone has these thoughts from time to time. I can even remember listening to a morning radio show once where they were talking and joking about obsessive thoughts. They said, "But you know you're not going to do it, it just pops into your head." Another person on the radio said, "I know I'm not going to do it, but sometimes I think, 'What if I run my car into that other car?'"

Obsessive thoughts are normal and most people have them. It's just that most people know to shrug them off. Or, in the case of the radio show hosts, laugh them off.

However, if you have panic attacks, that certainty you once had of knowing an obsessive thought is just something that pops into your head for no apparent reason is gone. You have no certainty anymore. Nevertheless, deep down, you know for certain you won't do this "bad" thing. But we stop believing and trusting in ourselves. So, we have to make sure we don't do it. One way to make sure you don't? Punish yourself, via a panic attack.

I believe, and this is only my opinion, that's one reason panic comes into play. Without an obsessive thought to spur one on, panic can't really operate. There has to be a reason for it to materialize. If you have a panic attack, it's assured you won't follow through on the obsessive thought. You stop worrying about the obsessive thought and concentrate on the panic. So, in a way, the panic takes the horror of what "might" happen away. "I can't think about that right now, I'm panicking." Sure, I say that with a certain amount of facetiousness, but it's true, isn't it?

So, you give into the panic to insure you don't do whatever obsessive thought you had. Obsessive thoughts keep us on edge because we do have a real fear that we're capable of doing "bad" things. But mostly what we fear is losing control. Of course, this gives the thought time to linger and sink in. The next thing you know, you're having a panic attack.

It's all about the fear of losing control. Obsessive thoughts, while normal, are a way for panic attack sufferers to engage their minds in a little war. And it starts by fighting the obsessive thought. If you can fight it off, you can keep it under control. But there's no fighting off obsessive thoughts because everyone has them at some time or another.

The trick here is to not get hung up on the obsessive thought. Call it what it is: An obsessive thought. You have to understand that it is just something that pops into your head, for whatever reason, not something that you're going to actually do. Once you let that thought linger, it has time to stir up trouble and to set off an attack. Once you begin to put too much emphasis on that thought and take it as the truth, you're going to have a panic attack whether you like it or not.

It happened to me a lot.

I can remember being on vacation in Florida once with my husband. We were in a tiny hotel room and getting ready to go to bed. Just before I drifted off, I thought, "What if I get up and hurt him? I could smash a lamp over his head." The thought sent me into a panic so bad I didn't get a wink of sleep all night. My heart was racing and I felt like throwing up. I tossed and turned and felt horrible—*How could I think something like that? I must be absolutely crazy!* The rest of the vacation was ruined because I was terrified I might lose control and do something terrible.

Realistically, I knew I wasn't capable of hurting him or anyone, for that matter. But when you have panic attacks, you don't rationalize; you really believe that you could lose control. That's why it's so important to remain rigid and vigilant at all times. When you're in the throes of a panic attack, the only thought you have is of getting that control back and never, ever losing it again.

Once I realized where most of my panic attacks originated—with obsessive thoughts—I began to see some light at the end of the tunnel. It was a small light but it was a light nonetheless. It was hard work trying to not panic after an obsessive thought and it's my opinion that people with panic attacks have a lot more obsessive thoughts than most. It did wear me down, but once I found that teeny tiny clue in all of this chaos, I knew I was headed in the right direction. It would take time, I knew, but it was a step closer to my goal—of eliminating panic from my life.

But the main thing was that I had recognized how important obsessive thoughts are in the process of panic. Once I did that, I was able to get the attacks under control. I had more control over them because I knew where they were coming from. And all I had to do was figure out how big a part obsessive thoughts were playing in my panic attacks. And it made complete sense. I would have an obsessive thought and then, after the thought, I'd get scared and then I'd have a panic attack. This turned out to be a clue that had been hidden from me. It was one of the things that helped me to turn in the right direction, though it took me a while for me to understand what the psychologist meant.

So I guess the visit to the psychologist wasn't wasted entirely. In fact, going to the psychologist was a step in the right direction because she clued me into my obsessive thoughts. After my first major panic attack, I realized obsessive thoughts were what brought my panic on. And it could have been a small thought, like getting a vitamin caught in my throat or choking on food or cutting my finger with a knife. Any thought in that direction of potential harm could set one off. But it's learning how to control these little thoughts and recognizing them for what they are that will help ease the panic.

Having said that, let me say this: Obsessive thoughts, in my opinion, *are only in reaction to your biggest fear.* They keep you from realizing what you're most afraid of. They are the proverbial man behind the curtain. They are the façade that holds tight and refuses to let you see the real truth.

Obsessive thoughts, combined with panic, are the only the shroud covering your biggest fear. Once you can remove the shroud, you can get to the fear and your panic will disappear.

That's why it's so important to find the strength and the will to face up to your biggest fear. Yes, you can control your panic attacks but if you never face the real issue you're having, they will always loom large over your head and threaten to come out and ruin your day. Sometimes, even your life.

No alternative.

The thing you have to realize is that you can't run, you can't hide and you can't outwit panic. You can't trick it nor can you wish it away. You have to face it head-on and you have to be strong.

You might think this is easier said than done. What isn't? But that's the great thing. This isn't hard to do. What's hard is to face the fear because, well, it *is* your greatest fear. This is where the buck stops.

It might not be as bad as you think it is, depending on your own circumstances. But is it worse than living like this? What's worse? Confronting your fear or letting that monkey ride your back for the rest of your life? It's your choice.

It's hard, I know. I've been though it myself. I know when you're having panic attacks, it's terrifying to even think about confronting the real issue. You think that it will make you even "crazier", that it will be what pushes you over the edge.

Believe me, I know this first-hand. And I also know that confronting your biggest fear is the only thing that works with panic. But you need to be aware of one thing that I have come to accept as the truth: *Panic comes from the repression of our fears.*

Also, our fears lie in the unfamiliar. With panic, familiarity breeds not contempt but necessity. It becomes necessary to stay home more often than not, to tune yourself out from something imaginary that might bring an attack on, such as a horror movie. As I've said, our world becomes smaller and smaller. What we need to realize is that the smaller it becomes, the harder it is for us to breathe.

But isn't it time? Isn't it time to step out into the world and live in it? Isn't it time to face the fear that keeps you in perpetual panic? It's your call, you know? It's your life and it's calling to you. It's ready for you to take it back from the clutches of panic.

So ask yourself this: What is the alternative? What is the alternative to not facing my fear? The alternative is a lifetime of panic. It's a lifetime of being on edge and wondering when panic will strike again.

That's what I did. The alternative was a lifetime filled with panic and with not living. Facing my fear, compared to that, seemed like an easy task. So, for me, there was no alternative but to face the fear.

This is how I got over panic attacks: I had to recognize my greatest fear and have the strength to call it up. It wasn't, for me, about living through it, it was about getting *to* it. It was about uncovering it.

It's learning how to get back to the one fear instead of circling around it. It's about being strong and calling it up from the dark recesses of your mind and staring it right in the face. Once you can do this, you can get over panic attacks.

The Big Bad.

Panic is a big monster that covers a little fear. It's all talk and no action. It's all smoke and no fire. We think it's worse than it really is. But many times, it's not. What we fear the most isn't The Big Bad lurking in the shadows or the thing that goes bump in the night.

We would rather not confront the source of our panic, sometimes to the point of disassociating ourselves from it. Sometimes we disown it by telling everyone that everything is "fine". All the while, inside, we regress. But panic comes up and forces us to realize that there is something deep inside of us that we're running from. It's chasing us and won't let us be. It's time that we face it head-on. Without facing it, it will continue to chase us.

After it's over, after we confront our deepest fear, the one that haunts us and makes us panic, we wonder why it got to us so much. Most times we come to the realization that this little fear, this little bully, doesn't have the power to harm us at all.

Are you ready to do just that? Then let's get to it.

Fear is a four-letter word.

Panic is all about fear. It's all about what you fear most. Panic is a way to deal with your fear without dealing with it directly. Panic scoots around the real issue and hides it from plain sight. This might be a lot to swallow but it's fear that's making you have panic attacks. You're not only overcoming panic attacks, you're overcoming the main force behind them—fear. Once you can get over your fears, you can free yourself of panic.

If there's nothing else you take from this book, please take that. And fear, while it can keep you safe, can also keep you from living. Sure, you'll exist and you'll probably keep your job and you'll get through the day. But you won't enjoy it very much.

Panic can hold you back and squeeze every bit of joy out of your life. Panic can freeze you; it can turn your life cold. You're not sure about anything anymore and everything has lost its meaning. It gets in your head and it never seems to get out. If you get lucky and forget about it for a while, it always comes right back. It just never seems to stop. It destroys your life.

You might ask yourself what happened. You used to be so self-assured, so happy. Nothing ever got to you. You were strong, a big personality. You had it all before panic and now all you can do is stand back and watch it all fall apart.

But you don't have to watch helplessly anymore. You don't have to put up with it. You can overcome it. But you have to be willing to get over it. You have to be willing to conjure up that fear and face it head on.

I'm going to tell you what I did to overcome it, step by step. You can try it, too, and see if it helps you. If at anytime it becomes too hard, you can stop. But just know until you get to that fear that's eating you up, you'll have to keep trying.

It's hard, I know. It's hard not to be terrified and to not quiver. It's hard not to want to run away. But no matter where you run, panic's gonna run with you. I know this firsthand. I know how hard it is to force yourself to sit and relax. I know how hard it is to confront a fear. But understand this part is the hardest. Once you can confront the fear, you'll feel much better and that's a pretty good thing.

But what if...
- You go crazy?
- You can't handle it?
- You hurt someone?
- You lose control?

Let me say it again: *You will not do these things.* These obsessive thoughts are only distractions. They are distracting you from doing the work you need to do to get over panic. They are nothing more than little pesky thoughts that keep you in a vicious cycle of panic. They are what you get hung up on so you won't take that big step. They are holding you back from reclaiming your life. They are your excuse not to move forward.

Look at it this way. If you were going to do something such as hurt someone else, wouldn't you have done it already? If you're *that* close to losing control, then a little thought like that isn't going to stop you. In fact, if you're going to lose control, you're not even going to have that thought. You'll already be off and you certainly wouldn't be reading this book.

And this is our main concern, losing control. That's why we imprison ourselves and hide under the bed. We're afraid of losing control. We think that anything might make us "freak out"—from a plane ride to a rollercoaster to an overnight trip. We believe that if something happens, we wouldn't be able to control ourselves and that means we might hurt someone or that something will happen to us.

Think about it, though. If you "freak out", what's the worst thing that could happen? You'd end up getting embarrassed or you might get kicked out of a restaurant or something. Many people have a fear of flying that's not about the plane crashing, but about being up in the air, out of control and susceptible to a panic attack. But the thing is we think the panic keeps us in control, that's why we have the attacks. If we gave in and "freaked out", as we all believe we are capable of doing, then panic would have no place in our lives. It is just a fear of losing control and that's why we have these thoughts—to keep us in line.

We mistakenly think these thoughts are what keep us from losing it. But they don't. They keep us in the dark, afraid of our own shadows, afraid to look for the real truth. That's because these thoughts are just a bunch of phony baloney. They want you to be afraid under the allure of "staying in control". They are what's keeping panic alive inside of you. These thoughts are controlling you. They control everything about you, from what you eat, to where you'll drive, to how long you can stay in the shower.

These thoughts are the blanket covering your fear. Throw them off. What good are they doing you? Not a damn bit. They are keeping you from uncovering the truth. They are a protective measure for your greatest fear. With these thoughts comes the certainly that you will never get to that fear. They are blocking you at every turn. Anytime you're close, doesn't one or two pop up to put you back into your panicked state?

Keep in mind that you are the one who is doing this to protect yourself from your fears. It's your thoughts that are keeping you from moving on, from taking that big step. And I know it's a big, big step. It's terrifying. But it has to be done. Without doing it, panic will rule over your world indefinitely. And the thing is, it doesn't have to rule. It's much easier to live without panic than to live with it. Believe me, I know this firsthand.

Still not convinced?

I'll tell you what I did. As I've said, I don't consider myself to be overtly religious but I do believe in God. So, what I did was pray. I closed my eyes and asked God to give me the strength to get through this. If you're not religious, you can still do this. What do you have to lose? It doesn't mean you're converting to a new faith or joining a cult or anything, it just means that you are trusting in a Higher Power. And, in my opinion, there's nothing wrong with that.

Keep in mind that before you do this, you're treating panic as a psychosomatic disorder, as I said in an earlier chapter. All psychosomatic disorders do is conveniently allow an "injury" to pop up so that you will not be able to face up to your fears. Remember, if you face up to your fears, your pain can go away. That's all you're doing is facing your fears to stop panic in its tracks. You probably think you have no idea what it is. But you do know. It's there, somewhere in your mind and it's ready to be faced so you can begin to live again.

Ready?

You will have to take some time. You need to be alone for this. Take a day or afternoon or morning or whatever you can muster off from work. It shouldn't take long but you will be a little tired afterwards, you might even cry—with relief. You'll also be very happy. You might even want to celebrate.

Now sit down someplace comfortable. It can be your couch or kitchen table, just somewhere you're comfortable. After you're comfortable, sit back and close your eyes. Take a few deep breaths and clear all the mumbo-jumbo out of your mind—that's the most important thing to do. It's almost a meditative stage you're going into. Tell yourself that you are going to relax for this space of time and then do that—relax. If you begin to feel panicky, *do not give into it*. Let it pass and then get focused on clearing your mind. You might have an obsessive thought or two, such as "What if I go crazy?" If you have a thought, that's fine, don't worry about it. Tell yourself that you will face the imagined consequences and trust in yourself.

Now say a little prayer. It doesn't have to be anything fancy, just something along the lines of, "God, I am going to do this. I need You to be there for me. Please help me to get though this. I am ready to face my greatest fear. Please tell me what my greatest fear is."

Now sit still. Wait for it to come to you. Don't force it. Just ask God to be with you and to let you know what your biggest fear is.

You might be a little scared and think that you will go crazy. *You won't.* Remember, that's just fear and the fear of having a panic attack is what might be keeping you from doing this. *It's just fear.* If you feel the fear, let it pass and then refocus. Keep in mind that fear can't hurt us but it can hinder us from getting better. *That's what it does.* Make it go on permanent vacation.

Just relax and let it occur to you. Your mind is clear and you're ready to do this. If you have a panic attack, that's okay. Most likely, you won't but if you do, just get through it and come back to center.

Face the fictitious consequences of "what if". Tell yourself if you "freak" out or "do something bad" or whatever, you'll deal with it. Allow yourself to trust yourself. Trusting in yourself is the biggie right now. Without the trust, it won't work. So, tell yourself that whatever happens afterwards is fine. If "they" have to do this or that, then that's what "they" have to do. Right now, *you* have to get to the root cause of your panic.

It's time to face your fear. After you have emptied your mind, let it occur to you. Ask yourself what your biggest fear is. "What is my biggest fear?" It should materialize shortly.

If it doesn't come, just stay relaxed and it will come. Be sure not to try too hard and stay focused. You have to let everything else go for this little space of time. Don't be afraid and trust the process. This means you have to trust yourself and God. If you're having trouble, just say a little prayer, asking God to stay with you and keep you strong. He will.

Keep in mind that if it doesn't work the first time, just relax and keep trying. It will occur to you. You already know what it is. All you're doing is uncovering it.

So what was it? Mine was I was afraid of being a failure. Yours might be something entirely different. But your fear isn't of the sky falling or driving off the road. Your fear, though it may sound silly to others, is what has been guiding you and bringing on the panic attacks. Once you realize that fear, your panic will go away. It's no big deal, you can handle it.

All you're doing is retracing your panic back to its beginnings. You have to be willing to accept any imagined consequences such as being carted off to the loony bin before you can face the fear. Tell yourself that it's okay. And face that fear. After you face it, you will wonder why you let it get to you. It got to you because it's your biggest fear, the deal-breaker. It's what pushed you to panic. Dealing with panic, your subconscious rationalizes, is easier than confronting your greatest fear and accepting inadequacies.

Perhaps your fear is a common one. Many people have them.

Common fears:
- Are you afraid you made a bad choice?
- Are you afraid you made a mistake and will have to deal with it the rest of your life?
- Are you afraid you regret something but can't name it because it's too hard to deal with and makes you into a "bad" person? This could be anything from having a baby to getting married to moving to switching jobs.
- Are you afraid you won't be able to take care of your family?
- Are you afraid that something might happen to your family?
- Are you afraid you're in a situation you can't escape from?

- Are you afraid you're a loser? A failure? A lost cause? Worthless? Unlovable? That you'll spend your life alone?
- Are you afraid everyone will find out you're a big fake? A fraud? (If this is the case, keep in mind that this is just an idea you put in your head because you feel as though you're not good enough. Insecurity gets to the best of us.)

The fear you have isn't something arbitrary but the feelings you have behind it are. And by this I mean they're unfounded fears. Facing up to them doesn't mean you are telling yourself you're a loser, it only means that you are facing them so you can name them, deal with them and then move on. It's just fear, that's all, and that's what you have to accept.

Whether you're afraid or not, the situation will continue to exist. So why waste time and effort being afraid? It's not doing anyone any good, especially not yourself. By dealing with this doesn't mean you *are* a failure or a fake or a loser or a bad mother or a bad wife or husband or whatever. It means you have a fear of being that way, nothing more.

Once and for all, once and for good, take this minute, one minute and face that fear. Whatever it may be, whatever it is holding you back. Stare that fear right in the face and let the thought sink into your brain. You know what? It's not so bad, is it? No, and in addition to that, it's liberating. Once you face it, feel the pressure release inside of you. Think of God reaching down and plucking that heavy railroad tie right off your shoulders, just as He did mine. You might just feel as though you had a religious experience. And, maybe, you have.

After you face your fear and let it go, you will never feel better in your life. That weight is gone and it doesn't have to come back. I know it sounds almost too simple. And that's because it *is* simple. It is easy to do.

Funny how that works.

The easy guide.

Here is an easy step-by-step guide to what I did in order to overcome my panic attacks and fear. I've done this as a quick reference so it will be easier to read once you get ready to do it.

The easy guide:
- Find a quiet place where you can be alone. (Be sure there are no distractions—kids, TV, etc.)
- Close your eyes and try to relax.
- Say a little prayer, if necessary, asking God to be with you and to help you face your fear.
- Face the fictitious consequences of "what if".
- When you're ready, ask yourself: What is my biggest fear?
- Let the answer occur to you. It should come quite easily but don't force it. (When it comes to you, you'll know for sure, so there's no skirting around it. When it's the right one, you will *feel* it. So, relax and *let it come*.)
- After you recognize your fear, the panic should subside.

Always keep in mind that this is an easy process, so don't make it harder than it is. It might be the fear of change that keeps us in the grip of panic. We might be afraid to let it go because it becomes so much a part of our lives that we wouldn't know what to do without it. However, no excuse is valid. It's time to get your life back. You can do that starting today.

The last time I panicked.

One of the main reasons I wrote this book is because not too long ago, I had a major panic attack doing something quite ordinary—driving.

The attack came out of nowhere. I had just been shopping and was driving on the interstate to go meet my husband for lunch. I had just gotten some really good deals on some stuff and that always puts me in a good mood. So, I was happy. I was driving along fine even though traffic was a bit heavy.

As I drove, I couldn't ever remember being as calm as I was then. I couldn't remember being so in tune with things, so confident. I was driving like an old pro, too. I was going along easy, a favorite CD in the player. I was so comfortable and relaxed that I realized I might just be a little *too* relaxed.

Then it hit me, panic, seemingly out of nowhere. Before I knew what was happening, I was experiencing a major attack. I hadn't had one like this in years. My nerves were tingling and my heart was palpitating. I was sweating, I was nauseous. My hands were shaking. I looked over my shoulder and saw that the last exit had just passed. I looked ahead and realized I was about to go up an enormous mountain, a scary mountain all the while stuck between two tractor-trailers.

The last time I panicked. 69

My thoughts turned to escape: I had to pull over. I had to turn back. I couldn't do this. Something could happen! I could go over the side of the mountain! A truck could hit me!

Then I realized:
- There was no going back.
- There was no escape.
- I was stuck.

Then my thoughts turned to the inevitable "what if". *What if something happened to me? What if I died? What if, what if, what if?*

I had no choice. I had to drive over that mountain. I took a breath, told myself to calm down and got in the right-hand lane. I got behind a slower moving vehicle and drove over that mountain, then down it. I drove all the way to my lunch destination and then I met my husband.

I got through it. But it wasn't good enough. I began to question it, analyze it, all the while not realizing that I was covering up the real reason for the attack. I kept asking myself, "Where did that come from?" and "Why did it come right now?" I kept worrying about it and, of course, it ruined my day and my lunch. I couldn't eat; I'd just had a panic attack out of nowhere. Where did it come from? What was the fear? What was I so afraid of?

Nothing came to mind.

Besides that, I was pissed off about having a panic attack. It seemed that every time I got my life in order and I began to feel more relaxed and happy, I got an attack. Why did this have to happen to me?

It took me a week to figure out what happened. And it was right in front of my face the entire time: I got a little scared about going over that mountain, and that little fear tricked me into a panic attack, making me doubt everything. It made me worry about "what" could happen. It made me fear things I hadn't feared in a long time and made me think these disconcerting thoughts:

- There was no going back.
- There was no escape.

You see, that's that way panic operates. It's fear, plain and simple. It tricks you into having panic attacks. It feeds on itself. Before you know it, it's spiraled out of control. Even though I searched for a bigger fear, it was a little fear that day that turned my world upside down.

The only reason I knew it was only a little fear that gave me a panic attack was because I remembered the last time I became panicked was on the cruise ship I mentioned earlier. On the ship, I wasn't afraid of an underlying issue, I was just afraid of being out in the middle of the ocean on a boat for days. When I stopped trying to figure it out, the thought came to me and that's when I knew it was just a little fear. It was a fear of not being able to escape a situation and being forced to see it through.

The fear dominated me and it also dominated my common sense and logic. Sure, something might happen but, really, what could I do about it? Nothing. If it happens, then I deal with it but I can't put my life on hold waiting for that unnamed, tragic thing.

So, you should keep in mind that you might have another attack here or there. Just learn to recognize them for what they are. Do not let the attack keep you from doing what you would normally do, or from challenging yourself.

If you do that, panic wins and in no time, you'll be back to having them everyday.

Also, remember that you're still here. That means panic has not won. You can overcome it. Just stick in there and wait it out and watch it disappear.

Life after panic.

While I say that the panic will subside, you should be aware that you might still feel a little on-edge sometimes. That's because now you have to start living without panic. It's a wonderful way to live, though. However, it's possible that you might feel a bit "empty" and have a feeling of "what's next?" You might also feel a little drained and with good reason. You've just been through a very exhausting experience. You will have to adjust. That's okay. It's part of the process.

I know that, for me, months after I got over my panic attacks and started living "normally" again, I felt empty. Not empty as in there was nothing inside of me anymore, but just tired. As I said, panic drains you emotionally and physically. I can remember just sitting around wondering what I was going to do now. I soon figured it out and the answer was easy: Live!

So, just be aware that you might have to readjust to your life after panic. But that's okay! It's a journey, so just hang tight and enjoy it afterwards. You're on the right path now, so stay on it and see it though to the end. There are a lot of things you'll have to do before you can get it all back. It does take time but it will come. The good thing is that it's stuff you already know, but have either forgotten or didn't realize you could do in the first place. Always remember to trust in the process.

Also, just be aware that you may experience another panic attack after you get through your fear. I like to call this "aftershocks". That simply means that after panic, you might feel a little jittery and on-edge and you might even have another attack here or there. That's okay. These panic attacks, from my experience, were less intense and easier to manage. What's important to keep in mind is that you can overcome them and you can do it by being aware of what triggers an attack and managing it, if and when one comes.

If at any time you feel that you might be slipping back into panic, just do what I do: Confront your feelings and ask yourself why you're feeling jittery. Once you can start to do this, your feelings of unease will dissipate. Soon, if and when you start to feel that tingly sensation that signals the start of a panic attack, you will know what's happening and what you can do to stop it. You will know it's a fear that's creeping up inside and that it's time to confront it head-on. Once you can make this a habit, you can be panic attack free.

Another thing I do is to just say no. That's right. Just say no to the threat of panic. You will probably have those feelings from time to time, but that doesn't mean you have to succumb to them. When you find yourself drifting into panic, fearing some event that's coming up in the days ahead, just stop thinking about it and tell yourself, "I will deal with it when it comes. Right now, I'm doing—whatever it is you're doing—and I need to concentrate." This applies to anything: Falling asleep, working, reading, whatever. Whenever you start to feel panicky, just say no. Sure, it is easier said than done, but once you start doing it, it will become second-nature.

On the other side of that, you can also say "yes" to panic. That's right, tell it to come on in. Stop and get ready for it. Call it up and make it make itself known. I know this sounds almost counterproductive, but if you think about it, saying "yes" really works and that's because you're telling it you're not going to wait for the attack, you want to go ahead and get it over now. This allows yourself to deal with panic and the great thing is, you don't have to deal with it once you say "yes". So, if you find yourself feeling a little jittery and fearing an attack, just tell panic to come on in. "Come on, let's get this over with. I don't have all day." Usually, it will go away almost instantaneously.

I have found that the more I resist panic, the stronger it becomes. So when I learned to stop resisting it so much, I was able to get over it. It's really that easy.

This is called building your strength. It's called facing the panic if and when it comes again. Don't fear it. Don't always be on the defense awaiting an attack. If you are constantly afraid of having an attack, then most likely, you *will* have an attack. Most of us feel "on-edge" at some time or another. It's no big deal. But we can learn to deal with it. All you have to do is find that courage inside and tap into it. Panic is like a bully. It picks on you and wears you down and makes you cower. But once you call a bully onto the floor, doesn't he usually back down? Yes, and so does panic.

Sure, you might have a panic attack again, like I did that day I was driving towards the mountain. It might hit you out of nowhere. But that doesn't mean you're going to have to live with it forever. *It's just a temporary discomfort.* Live through it, sort out your feelings on it and then confront the fear. Then move on. Don't let it become a stumbling block that puts you back into panic's arms. You know for a fact that you've lived through them before so what's the big deal? After a while, it does become more of an inconvenience than anything else. You need to learn to look at it this way. Don't make it bigger than what it is.

Building your strength is the best way to eliminate panic. And you do that by taking chances by going on a plane or vacation or whatever. You will feel a bit on-edge thinking about the upcoming event, but if you force yourself through it, you will soon realize it's no big deal. If I feel nervous about something, I think to myself, "I'll just do it and let whatever will be, be." What you are doing by doing this is building a stronger foundation. It was once wobbly but now you're replacing the old blocks with newer, better and stronger ones. It's all about trust. Trust yourself to do the right thing and you will.

Remember that fear is always the culprit in panic. It's fear that brings panic on but it's strength in confronting the fear that sends it away. The worst thing you can do is to not recognize this. Remember, most of the cure of anything lies in the recognition of the problem and the problem lives in the symptoms.

Soon, though it may take a few months, you might look back at your panic attack experience and wonder if that was even you. I know I did. I'd shake my head and wonder how I lived like that. But then I thank God for getting me through it.

Whatever you do, just keep in mind that this experience will make you a better person. It will possibly even make you more sensitive to others. Maybe you can be there for someone who is going through panic attacks and you can help them.

Also, this experience will make you a stronger person. There are things that you only dreamed about that will become a reality for you once you gain your strength. For me it was going to Europe. Before, I always had an excuse of why "not to" go. There wasn't enough money or time or whatever. One day, my husband and I sat down and decided it was time. And we went. The moment I laid eyes on the Eiffel Tower, I realized how strong I was. And without panic, I might not have ever done that. I would have kept putting it off until one day it would have totally disappeared from my mind. It would have been one of those things that I would "get around to someday", though I would have never gotten around to it.

Because of panic, I look forward to new experiences. Mainly because I want to test myself and see how strong I truly am. This is not to say I would do anything like bungee jumping or skydiving. That's just a little too dangerous for me—even before panic. And I'm still not a big fan of big rollercoasters, though I will get on the smaller ones. But it doesn't matter. I still test myself without going overboard. There's no reason, in my mind, to go overboard.

We all have our balance and we all have things we like and don't like. I love to travel and panic almost took that away with me. But you know what? I've traveled *more* since panic than before. I make it a priority. The great thing about panic is that afterwards, you do prioritize. Maybe it's time for you to travel, too. If you can get to Paris, be sure to take a picture of the Eiffel Tower and put it up on your wall. If you can't, put a picture of it up there anyway. That picture will be a testament to your resilience and inner strength or to a goal that you have to get there. It will also be a testament to your faith. It means you are setting yourself on the right track again. It's a reminder that good things are on the way and that's because you're going to jumpstart them.

Always keep in mind that *you are a lot stronger than you ever thought.* There's no stopping you from doing what you truly want to do. If you can get through panic attacks, you can get through *anything*. Stop fearing "something" might bring an attack on. Stop looking for a life with just some of the edge taken off, a life that is just a tad less anxiety ridden. That's only settling for less than you deserve. You can start looking for beauty and love again, like you used to when you weren't consumed with panic. You can start building your dreams again and working towards them.

And, perhaps, that's what we're all afraid of. Maybe we're afraid of just trying. Because without panic comes the choice to get up and to do. If we're consumed with panic, we don't have to move out of our comfort zone. All we can truly deal with when we have panic attacks *is* panic. As strange as it may sound giving that up might be a fear, too. What will you do then? Where will you go when panic isn't an excuse anymore? Sometimes, it's almost too much to bear.

But that prison you're living in keeps getting smaller and smaller. It keeps getting easier and easier to avoid situations. It's no way to live.

Your life is there, waiting for you. Sure, you got detoured but now it's time to get back on track. Sit down and write out the things you really want to do. If you want to go back to college or get a new job, go for it. Getting over panic attacks will give you more courage than you ever thought you had. Now you know that the worst thing that can happen is that you could fail. Failing isn't so bad because with each failure comes a little more confidence and maybe even a better way to do things. Fear of failing is nothing compared to panic attacks. Who cares about failing after you get though that? It doesn't even seem to matter. And that means it frees you up *to try*. And with trying always comes some sort of gratification: I gave it my best. Now I can move on.

What a gift.

Knock wood.

With panic, I acquired a bad obsessive/compulsive habit: Knocking wood. When actual wood wasn't available, I would knock on my head. I know it sounds crazy. I'm sure it looked even crazier.

But that's what panic does. It gives us new things to obsess about. Sometimes, we get a little obsessive/compulsive habit to go along with it. If you've acquired one, don't feel too bad over it. If you can get over your panic, more than likely, this little habit will disappear or decrease greatly.

When I was having panic attacks, I would feel like a fool, but I had to do it, I had to knock wood. I still do it, though not as much. It's a hard habit to overcome. And that's because there is still a little bit of the fear inside of me.

A little fear, in my opinion, isn't necessarily a bad thing. A little fear keeps us from making mistakes and acting foolish. It's just that we have to recognize when it's going overboard, such as checking and re-checking the lights and stove before we leave the house. Sometimes, you have to take control of it and say "no more". It's hard because you're still in the thought pattern of believing that you have to control everything and if you make one mistake, your whole world could come tumbling down. And checking things or knocking wood gives us a sense of security.

But the security is false. We're not in control. That's the biggest lesson panic gave me and no matter how many times I knock wood, I can't control what "might happen". Hate to tell you, but you can't either.

The world at large is out of our control and learning to accept that we don't have control over what happens is one of the biggest favors we can do for ourselves. It opens us up and helps us to enjoy our days more. It takes the responsibility off our shoulders and, let's be honest, most people with panic attacks tend to carry the weight of the world on their shoulders.

I know I did. I would worry and fret over people at my job and my family. I would want the best for them and I would offer advice and help when I could. When something "bad" would happen, I'd feel somehow at fault for it, thinking I could have done more, offered more, been around more.

But in reality, I did what I could. In fact, I went above and beyond the call of duty on more than one occasion. When I was finally able to realize I wasn't responsible for anyone but me, I began to feel happier and more alive than I ever had. And that's because I finally understood that I can't control things. Bad habits like knocking wood are just denial. It's just us thinking that we're in control. It's almost funny when you get right down to it.

The world is a big, big place. We are but small humans on this planet. We readily accept the "fact" that we're in control because we think we're more important than we really are. And no one is control, not even world leaders. God is in control and we have no control over that.

So I say, let it go. Just once don't double or triple check the stove. Check it once and make a point to pay attention to what you're doing and remember checking it. And then leave the house. Put the control in God's hands. That's where it belongs.

By doing this, you free yourself of the weight of the world. You free yourself of bad little habits like knocking on wood. You free yourself to a better existence. You free yourself of the panic. And isn't that what you want? All you have to do to get it is to surrender control. Stop being so rigid. Stop being a worrywart. And just start being you. That's all anyone wants.

Exposing yourself to the elements.

While I was having panic attacks, I stopped doing a lot of things I enjoyed. I stopped watching horror movies, or even TV series' that might have some gore in them. I stopped doing a lot of the things I once held dear. In essence, the person who liked certain things disappeared and this new person who was afraid of her own shadow emerged.

It's not like that now.

Panic won for a while but I gradually took my life back. I did that by exposing myself bit by bit to things. One of the best things I did was to start watching the TV show *Buffy the Vampire Slayer*. I had refused to watch it before because I was terrified something in that show would set off an attack. But, because I found the show so interesting, I would find myself stopping on it occasionally and watching five or ten minutes, to the point that I thought I couldn't "take it anymore". Then I'd turn it off. Soon, I found myself so involved with the storyline that I didn't care what monster popped up on the TV. I would find myself rooting for the characters to get the "bad guy". It was like not being scared had crept up on me the same way being afraid had done. It was almost a complete role-reversal.

Another thing I did was to test myself. As with TV, I banned all horror movies in our house. The thought of watching a scary movie was too much. But I've always liked horror movies and I really missed watching them. So, I told myself that I could watch them—but only during the day. Then, bit by bit I got to the point that I could watch them at night.

Before panic, one of my most favorite activities was to read crime/mystery novels. After panic, I couldn't even read the back covers of these books. But soon, I did. I'd tell myself I'd read to the point that I couldn't take it anymore, then I wouldn't have to read anymore. Soon, I could read whole books again. That was one pleasure I really enjoyed rediscovering.

After I started panicking, something else I did, much to the chagrin of my husband, was to get rid of a lot of things in our house that made me uneasy, even knickknacks. We also had some books on superstition and things like that that had to go. I thought just having these books around might make something bad happen. After I got over panic attacks, I made a point to re-purchase some of these books. Panic may have forced things that were once interesting and entertaining out of my life, but no more. From then on, if I found something interesting, I'd get it. It was more just to prove to myself that things like this had no power over me and letting them have any power was downright silly.

Plane rides were a big no-no as well. But my husband and I really wanted to go to Las Vegas one year. I told myself no over and over but my husband pleaded with me to do it. I even went as far to tell him to go by himself, that's how badly I didn't want to get on a plane. But then, he talked me into it.

As we were entering the airport, I almost wanted to scream at him, "How did I let you talk me into this?!" But I kept my calm. I kept telling myself that if I wanted to leave, I could. I got through the airport and to my gate that way. We sat down and waited. When the attendant told us we could begin boarding, I didn't think about it. I pushed everything out of my mind and just walked down the ramp, found my seat and put my seatbelt on. Sure, I was nervous but I focused on a magazine I'd bought. I didn't tell myself I was going to freak out and panic, I just didn't think about it. When the plane took off, I got uneasy and almost wanted out, but I knew this was impossible, it was too late. I had to ride that plane. And when we were in the air, I calmed down and actually enjoyed it a little. Not a lot but a little.

That trip to Vegas was the best trip of my life. No, I didn't win big money, but I won big confidence points with myself. That trip is invaluable to me.

Another thing I became frightened of was swallowing pills. I was terrified one would get caught in my throat. I would only swallow one if my husband was around so he could help me if it happened. However, one day I had a terrible headache when I was by myself. The aspirin in the cabinet loomed larger than life. I finally said to hell with it and, with shaking hands, took the bottle out, got some water and swallowed a pill.

One last thing I did was to make sure I was always home before dark. I didn't want to go see movies at night or even go to dinner. Little by little, I made myself go out later and later. Soon, being out at night wasn't a big deal.

Before panic, I hated the idea of being alone in my house. While I would sometimes be alone at the house, I hated taking a shower without my husband there, so I'd always wait till night to take them. It was just a fear I had. I know now it was because panic was always creeping around me, teasing me, waiting to come out. Now, I'm happy to say, I can take my shower at any time during the day. If I get anxious about it, I turn the radio on and sing along with it until the feeling dissipates.

I like to call this process "exposing yourself to the elements". It's like I had to integrate myself back into my world little by little and that's what I did. I got a little exposure here and there until I could handle it all. With panic, our own worlds become unfamiliar and scary but once we get over it, we can start doing the things we once loved. What's so great about this is that we might even discover a few things we had forgotten about loving in the first place. It's wonderful to rediscover something.

Panic can occur anywhere and it sometimes takes us by surprise. When it does, just stay strong and remember that it is just a temporary discomfort you are feeling. And go do the activities you once enjoyed so much. Expose yourself bit by bit and before long, you'll be living large.

The biggest fear of all—death.

I wanted to include this chapter on death but I didn't want to put it in at first because I didn't want to scare anyone off. Yes, I know how terrifying this subject is. But I think it bears mentioning that another thing we're all afraid of is death. It's not a pretty subject but one that I wanted to touch on because, when I was having panic attacks, death was one of my biggest fears. In fact, when I would even start to think about it, it would set my recovery back.

If you don't want to deal with this right now, then just skip this chapter. But maybe if you open up a little and allow yourself just to read, then you might take a step in the right direction and get over the panic sooner.

When we're having panic attacks, we constantly think about death. Or, rather, we try to force thoughts about it out of our minds. This is a biggie for many of us. I know that if you just read that sentence, you might be feeling panicky; maybe you're even cursing me for bringing it up. If you are, just stop for a minute and take a breath. It's not as scary as we build it up to be, this subject of death. And if the subject is enough to bring on an attack or enough to make you curse, it's time to find out what your fear about it is. Maybe it's time to start asking questions about it, the first being, "Why am I so terrified of this?"

I know that, for me, before panic, I accepted that death is part of life. After, I began to really fear it. One day I realized that I would someday pass on. This realization terrified me and increased my panic attacks. I can remember thinking about death and just shaking at the thought of it. I told my husband one day, "I'm going to die one day. I'll be gone." And he nodded and said, "We all are."

This realization was a hard pill to swallow. Maybe one reason we're so sensitive to the subject of death is because during an attack, we feel close to it. Of course, we're not, but when a person's heart is palpitating, it makes one all the more fearful.

I believe we all have a fear of death because it is the "great unknown". For me, my faith helps with this. Other faiths talk of reincarnation and things like that. I think having faith in a Higher Power is key here. Being able to tap into your faith and talk to God is one way to gain some reassurance.

The fear of death is a harder fear to get over because it is rooted in reality. But, for me, just accepting that death is a natural part of life was the way to get through this enormous fear. It took a while, but I did it. When a thought about death would occur to me, I'd just deal with it and then let it go. These thoughts are scary but, as I said, learning to accept it is the way to get over it. I believe that you can never learn how to live until you accept that you're going to die.

But the thought of death is enough to make us stop living, isn't it? And isn't that ironic? We use this fear as a protective measure, pulling the blanket over our heads and taking on new fears just to keep it at a distance. We stop taking "risks," some of us even stop going outside our houses.

We can't do this or that because of our fear of death; thusly we give up control of our lives over to this impending fear. Perhaps all panic is rooted in the fear of death. It is a biggie, after all. We give up our lives so we can keep them. It's really sort of ridiculous.

If we are constantly afraid of something happening, afraid that we're going to die, we're not really living. We're existing, calculating, hiding. We're praying that we'll get out of it. It's a hard fact to face, but none of us do. I know that during my time dealing with this, I wouldn't watch horror movies, as I mentioned before, because they all deal with death and that was a reminder that one day I'd have to deal with it, too.

In today's world, the fear of death is huge, even though we have new inventions and ways to extend lifetimes. Perhaps we all have an unhealthy preoccupation with it. It's always on the news, always being talked about. And this keeps it on our minds constantly.

When I was dealing with this, I started to think about things and I came to this conclusion about death: Perhaps we're not really afraid of death but of living. Panic makes us afraid of living so dealing with death on top of that makes it all the more frightening. That's when we start trying to "protect" ourselves from it. We stop doing this or that. But what we're really stopping is our joy of living. That's what panic does and it brings death into the equation. In fact, it just sort of slips in there one day and it increases the fear of every single thing.

Now you're really not living, are you? Now you're really worrying all the time about everything, including death, and that means you're not living at all.

The only way to get over this fear is to just accept that we are all going to die. Yes, I know how that sentence sends tingles up and down your spine and I know how hard it is to do that very thing. But without acceptance, you can't get over panic. One day, it will stop bothering you so much. But don't wait for that day. Take action now and start learning how to live again. You have to resign yourself to the fact that you're going to die and try to have as good a life as possible before it happens. If nothing else, acceptance may help you to prioritize and start doing the things you've always put off doing because we all only have a certain amount of time on the earth. Realizing this isn't a curse and it doesn't have to be overwhelming. It can be used as a tool in helping us to get to the things we all want such as getting married or having kids or traveling or whatever.

It's a harsh reality but it's inevitable. We think if we stop accepting it, then we can do something about it but we can't. That's why we become so afraid to get on the rollercoaster or the airplane or whatever. We take precautions that just keep us from living. We think we're sidestepping death, but we're not. It's going to get us eventually anyway. What we're really doing is sidestepping life.

Another thing I did was to start asking questions and to start studying death—not in a morbid way, mind you. I just started reading and being more open to the subject, that's all. There is a great amount of resources out there for this very thing. Why not learn everything you can about it? I'm not saying to become obsessed with it, but why not open that door up a little? If you can do this, you can learn to accept this great consequence we all have to face. The more you allow your conscious mind to accept this, the easier dealing with it will become. And that's what it's all about—acceptance. I know it's hard. As I said, the very thought of death for me was enough to start a panic attack. But I learned to accept it and I learned to live with it. And so can you.

Death is scary for all of us. But, as I said, maybe our real fear is rooted in living, in not taking chances. And getting to real fear is what we're after. Once we can confront it, it stops controlling us and our fear of death, among other things, stops terrifying us, too.

The "reason" for panic?

For me, the reason for panic was that I was working too hard, trying too hard. I put off my mental well-being in favor of hard work and the allure of success. I thought success was a lighthouse in the night on a stormy ocean. All I had to do was swim through the current to get at it and then I'd be happy, safe and content. I thought that, through success, all my hopes and dreams would come true and I could finally be the person I always wanted to be. But the current was choppy and dangerous. It was all I had. I thought I had no way out of the current and I had to keep swimming, trying my best to find myself when, all along, I was there, right there, and all I had to do was open my eyes a little and see all that I had.

I don't believe that panic just comes out of the blue. I believe it comes for a reason. It comes to show us the way. Your life is calling and it doesn't want to be put on hold.

Panic was a wake-up call for me. It may have hit me like a ton of bricks but it has made me more grateful for what I have, for what I have accomplished. It was a reminder that I have it good and that everything's alright. Panic made me see things that I might not have ever seen before. It opened my eyes in a way that nothing else ever could have.

For you, your reason for panic may be different. It might have started in your childhood. It might be caused by something that happened in your family. It might have been a traumatic event, like an automobile accident or something similar. You might not think you know the reason for it, but you do. Look deep inside and let it occur to you. This will free you.

Life does have a way of throwing us curveballs. It is a series of ups and downs, just like everyone says. With panic, it seems, it's all down. But it doesn't have to be that way. Life can start to look up again, if you just give it a chance. All you have to do is be willing to give life a chance again, be willing to give up control and open your eyes.

In a way, I view panic as hiding. I think of it as hiding in clear sight. As I've said, it distorts everything but at the same time, it keeps us sheltered, doesn't it? You may scoff at that, but think about it. If you have panic as a constant threat, a constant danger, there is no danger you will do anything wrong. Panic keeps us in state of fear but at the same time, it's our excuse not to face up to what really scares us.

Panic keeps us from potential threats. It keeps us safe, in a way, because with panic, you won't ever step out of bounds and try something new. And the thought of stepping out of bounds is enough to send the terror in. *I can't do that! It might give me a panic attack.*

But panic is not a safe haven. It is living terror, a living nightmare. Consider the alternative. Live with panic or live without panic? It's a choice, in my opinion, it's just a choice. I chose not to live with panic. I chose to get my life back, to get a better life. You can do the same thing.

It is frightening to give panic up and face the things you need to face. So, don't go it alone. Ask God to help you. Ask your best friend or simply ask yourself to be strong. There are many people who are willing to hold your hand through this. But know you have to stop leaning at sometime, stand on your own two feet, square your shoulders and tell panic to do its worse. You are going to face what you need to face. You are going to call that fear up. Panic is simply standing in your way. Make it step aside and see how easy it is to get what is rightfully yours back.

We might just want it to be more complicated when, in fact, the answers are fairly simple. There's no need to make it harder than it already is. It's about taking the matter into your own hands and finding your own way out of panic, like I did. I believe we rely too heavily on "professionals" when most of the time the real truth we need is inside of us, waiting to be discovered. God gave us the ability to reason. He gave us insight and wisdom for a reason. He gave it to us so we can help ourselves.

We are strong. We just sometimes have to be reminded of that and panic is a reminder of how strong we really are. We're also very resilient creatures. We can come out of anything. We can do it. And all we have to do is call up the reserves inside each and every one of us. They're there, your reserve strength and your resilience. Call them up and let them aid you. That's what they're there for. And little by little, as you get stronger, add to the reserve. But know you will never deplete your reserves. They will be there to help you through anything.

Always be gentle with yourself. Always be kind to yourself. Treat yourself as a child you love and care for. Be caring. You are all you have. Be good to that person you are and give yourself the chance to see the light of day again. Take that chance and step out of the darkness. Or decide that you're not going to swim against the current anymore.

Maybe just let the current carry you to your safe haven. Its waiting, your safe haven, and it will open its arms and embrace you once you're ready to take that step. Don't ever doubt its existence.

Get back.

You can get back the life panic took away from you. But what's the fun in that?

Sure, you can go back to being the person you were before. But think about that person. Who were you? If you were like me, you were so focused on your career or whatever that you didn't do anything *but* work. You didn't stop and smell the roses and you never took an afternoon off. If you were like me, you didn't enjoy your family or your spouse or your home. It was all about doing better, getting more, succeeding. If you were like me, doing just that forced panic into your life and made you sit up and take notice that life was passing you by as you made plans for the future.

Panic is giving you the opportunity to do better, to be better, to see more clearly. Panic gave me a new set of eyes. I started seeing how beautiful things are, how wonderful life really is, and how lucky I was to be alive. That's why I say it was a gift. It was hell on earth for a period of time, but panic has helped me to bring everything that is really important into focus. It has made me appreciate what I have instead of longing for something else, for something better.

I have found that while, sometimes, the world does us "wrong", all we have to do is wait around until it does us right again. And it will, if you give it time.

I still dream. I still fantasize. But I don't let my lust for success run my life anymore. Sure, like everyone else, I want to succeed and I want to be happy. But my whole life isn't dedicated to this one thing that I think will make, or, if I don't get it, break me. There is no one thing that makes or breaks us unless we let it. This stuff only adds to our existence and experience.

We live in a very anxious world today. It's all about working hard and doing your best. It's about success, success, success—at any cost. And that cost is sometimes your mental health. The world we live in is very anxiety-provoking. It's about alarm clocks and bosses and time management. Rest isn't an option for many. Society expects way too much of us these days. We're constantly supposed to be doing and going—for our families, for our jobs, for our friends, for the community. People rarely get a break and most of us won't take one, normally out of guilt.

But I ask why should it matter if you sit on the couch all day every once in a while? What does it matter if all you do that day is flip channels and eat popcorn? It shouldn't but it does. We can't do that. We have bills to pay, babies to burp and people to please.

Before panic, that's all I was concentrated on, doing for others and rarely doing for myself. In addition to that, I spent a lot of time on my goals of finishing college and getting a better job and all that. After panic, not so much. Panic helped me reclaim my life and it helped me to re-focus. I realized that a job wasn't the sum-total of my existence. In fact, it's really just a paycheck. I realized that while a higher education is all well and good, it wasn't what I really wanted out of life. What I wanted, I realized, was just to have fun every once in a while. I wanted to relax and to laugh and to just be who I am. And that's what I set out to do—reclaim my time and myself.

If I don't feel like doing something on my off day, I just don't do it. If it "hurts" someone's feelings, they can just get over it. I know that if I never take time out—like I used to—I will become anxious and agitated. Without my free time, I would never be calm and collected.

Do what I did. Reclaim your free time and do whatever you want to do. Even if it's a day of channel surfing. Hey, you might be lucky and live near a beach and be able to do some real surfing. Who knows? But every once in a while, stake a claim in your off day and do whatever you want to do. It's for you and for your mental heath. Who cares if the windows need washing? They'll still be dirty next week.

However, most of us know that our lives will never be worry-free. We'd have to be cold individuals for that to happen. But we can live without panic attacks. We can live without the constant threat of one.

As Franklin Roosevelt said, "There is nothing to fear but fear itself." He was right. Fear is the enemy. It's not the actual imagined things we fear—driving over a mountain, plane rides, etc.—it's just the fear of being a failure or whatever. It's the "what if" and the "what if" is just fear. That's all it is. *It's just fear.* A stumbling block distorting our view of reality. A misrepresentation of reality that warps our perspective.

And, lastly, let what happened in the past stay in the past. Just because you dealt with panic on a daily basis doesn't meant you always have to deal with panic. Another thing, don't go back and try to relive it. Don't over-analyze it. Just take it for something that was in your life once that you got though.

Orson Welles said something really great once and I believe we can all learn a lesson from it. He said, "We all live with our pasts but I encourage it not to misbehave." Always remember what you've been through but never let it taint your today.

That's all I can give you. I hope this book has done you a world of good, I really, really do. I know when I was having panic attacks, I just wanted someone to tell me a way out. But I had to find the way out myself, with God's help. I hope this book can give you the way out you need. I hope it can bring you peace and understanding. And, lastly, I hope it can ease your mind so that you can get a good night's rest. That's something we can all use. Use it well and never take it for granted. And be happy that you made it though. You are, truly, stronger than you give yourself credit for.

Peace be with you.

Printed in the United States
42051LVS00007BA/23